Rugs and Carpets of the Orient

Knut Larson

FREDERICK WARNE · LONDON · NEW YORK

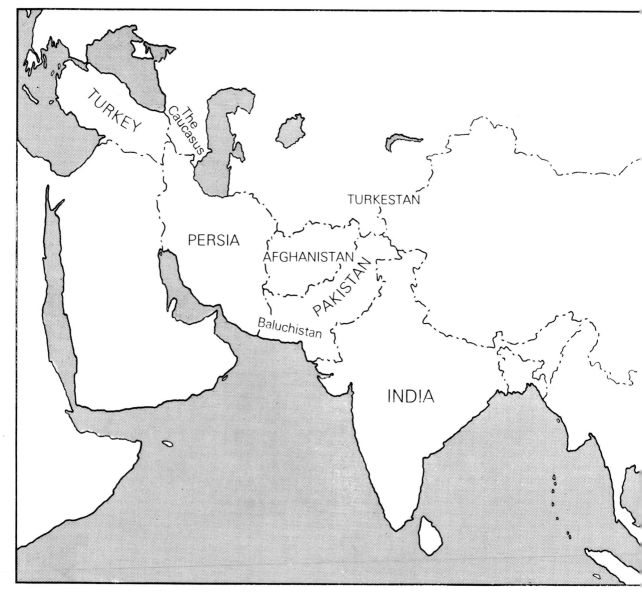

Countries and regions of the Orient where carpets are produced.

First Published 1962

© Nordisk Rotogravyr and Knut Larson 1962

English Translation © 1966 Frederick Warne and Co. Ltd., London, England

Printed in England by Henry Stone & Son (Printers) Ltd., Banbury, Oxon. 1978

Revised Edition © Frederick Warne (Publishers) Ltd., London, 1978

NA

CONTENTS

THIS BOOK is intended as a guide to greater knowledge of the oriental rug. It is not a tale about the mysteries of the East but a factual account of rugs and their manufacture, from the very first preparatory work to the final trimming of the finished rug.

In the forty or so years during which I have worked with oriental rugs and been in contact with customers, I have often heard requests for a factual and, above all, up-to-date handbook on oriental rugs. It is this request I have tried to meet by imparting the knowledge and experience which the study of hundreds of thousands of rugs during the years has given me.

I am often asked how one can learn about oriental rugs; how to distinguish between the different types and qualities. My answer is always the same: study rugs—at exhibitions and in specialist shops where there are people to answer your questions; try to see and feel as many rugs as possible and try to remember details of the rugs you study. Wool and technique are the most important distinguishing marks between rugs from different manufacturing districts.

It is, however, just as important to acquire theoretical knowledge from suitable literature on rugs. There are many excellent works in English and German, though many of these are chiefly concerned with antique rugs while the layman is primarily interested in the rugs that appear in the shops.

Of course one can never stop learning. Specialists will give different answers to the same question. One's own judgement combined with theoretical knowledge must then decide what is correct. It is necessary to have many years experience, to have travelled in countries where the rugs are made, and above all to be intensely interested in studying techniques and details if one is to be well versed in this trade.

Public interest in hand-knotted oriental rugs is steadily increasing. Consequently I consider it to be vitally important that the general public learns something about these rugs in order not to be deceived by the talk of unscrupulous salesmen; tales about certain rugs having been manufactured once upon a time for royalty or some high official are generally pure myths.

Thus, when buying a rug, go only to reputable shops where you can reckon on expert knowledge and well-tried experience; in this way you have a guarantee for both the product and the price.

I very much hope that this book will be frequently used. Even though one may not fill the entire house with rugs, this subject is so interesting that just knowing a little about the skills practised in the Orient to produce something beautiful and durable lends charm to even the simplest rug.

Knut Larson

A reconstruction of the Pazyryk carpet, approx. 2,400 years old. The original, which is only partly preserved, is now in the Hermitage, Leningrad.

THE ORIENTAL RUG has ancient traditions. It is not known when and where rugs were first made but it was certainly in prehistoric times. The oldest rugs probably had no pile; they were probably smooth like Kelim or Sumakh rugs, as far as can be told from archaeological excavations of the Pharaohs' burial chambers.

However, a knotted rug, approximately 2,500 years old, was found during excavations in the Altai mountains near the border of Mongolia. This rug, known as the Pazyryk rug, is almost square and measures approximately 6 ft. 3 in. × 6 ft. 4 in. or 190×200 cm. It is made with the Ghiordes knot, and the pattern consists of a central field broken up into small squares and surrounded by borders with horsemen and animals. Considering its great age, the greater part of this rug is in surprisingly good shape.

Rugs are depicted on several reliefs that are more than 2,000 years old. There is one in Persepolis, which shows an ambassador from a foreign power presenting rugs as a gift to the Persian King. Ancient writings also testify that knotted rugs were to be found in palaces and temples in most oriental countries.

Among the ancient rugs that still exist mention can be made of 13th-century rugs in the Ala-ed-din mosque in Konya, Asia Minor, and the Ming and Marby rugs from the 15th century. The last can now be found in the Statens Historiska Museum, Stockholm.

It was only natural that the nomads of the past needed rugs, both for protection from the cold and as an ornament in their tents. In those days the rugs had relatively simple patterns with repeating geometrical or stylized designs. The material for the pile was wool, goats' hair, camels' hair and occasionally silk. Gold and silver threads and precious stones were included in the finest rugs intended for royal palaces and temples.

DEVELOPMENT

The reign of Shah Abbas in Persia in the late 16th and early 17th centuries was one of the most important periods in the history of carpets. The Shah understood and encouraged the manufacture of rugs, organized large court factories and obtained outstanding artists who composed wonderful patterns with flowers and figures that are still being woven today, nearly 400 years later. Shah Abbas'

The Ardabil Carpet
17 ft. 5 in. ×34 ft. 5 in. approx.
(530 × 1,050 cm.).
Made in 1540. Victoria and Albert Museum, London.

The Marby Rug
3 ft. 7 in. ×4 ft. 9 in. approx.
(109 × 145 cm.).
15th century. Now in the Statens Historiska Museum, Stockholm.

father, Shah Tahmasp, had the famous Ardabil carpet made, which is now in the Victoria and Albert Museum in London and is regarded as one of the most magnificent rugs in the world. It measures approximately 17 ft. 5 in. ×34 ft. 5 in. or 5.30 × 10.50 metres, is quite tightly woven, has about 32,500,000 knots, a warp and weft of silk and the Sehna type of knot, i.e., the Persian knot. According to the inscription on the carpet it was woven by Maksud of Kashan, slave of the Temple. This is one of a pair; the other carpet is in the Los Angeles County Museum of Art.

Other rugs from this time are a magnificent example in silk belonging to the Swedish Royal family and the Danish "Coronation Rug" in Copenhagen.

Quality, charm of design, lively colouring and excellent handicraft characterize these rugs and make them works of art of the highest order. After the death of Shah Abbas carpets had a chequered history. It is true to say that the standard of rug production was highly dependent on the interest shown by the reigning prince. The continuous feuds and wars, with frequent changes of ruler, prevented much interest being paid to this industry.

NEW DYES

The majority of early dyes were vegetable. The first attempts to produce completely new ones came in the late 19th century, with the range of chrome dyes; these, however, were not fast.

Aniline dyes, from coal tar, were manufactured commercially about 1860, and were immediately exported to the East where they met a long felt want for certain colours not obtainable from the natural dyes then available. These colours were a deep purple, bright green, strong pink, mauve and a bright yellow.

It is understandable that the rug-maker was attracted by the new dyes. They saved him the time-consuming process of extracting his dyes from animals and plants, while the actual process of dyeing was both simpler and more convenient; but they were not very waterproof and they tended to fade in the light. In time the Persian authorities prohibited their use.

Later synthetic dyes reproduced the older vegetable ones such as indigo and madder.

Modern chemical dyes are highly sophisticated compounds produced with a known degree of light-fastness which is measured according to an international standard.

PRODUCTION

From the end of the 19th century the demand for oriental rugs rose sharply and exports to other parts of the world shot up. In Turkey a completely new rug production was organized, in sizes more suitable for contemporary requirements. Persian patterns were copied, the weaving was coarse, patterns and colours became stereotyped. The more important types among these new rugs came to be known as Ushak (the name of an important group of carpets dating from the 16th-17th centuries), Eskisher, Sparta and Ghiordes (where some of the finest prayer rugs had been made in the 18th century).

In Persia, too, at this time an English business concern started to organize factories in Tabriz as well as in Sultanabad, present-day Arak. They were followed by other European and American companies who also started production in different parts of Persia. This new form of manufacture produced new qualities and patterns and above all standardized sizes to certain dimensions suitable for Europe and America.

Since the second world war, a number of new problems have arisen in manufacturing carpets in Persia. The industry has expanded enormously and absorbed both labour and raw materials. Wages have risen and with them the standard of living. The price of wool is now a more important factor than it was, as a result of the industry's increased demand for this material.

All this has forced the factories to rationalize production, to concentrate on a limited number of different qualities in respect of both density and wool quality, and to spin and dye the wool in larger batches (unless spinning and dyeing are done at the weaving station) in order to reduce the cost of transport. Even so, rugs are still being made in all qualities, from simple, cheap bazaar rugs to the highest grades. Thus in Tabriz or Kerman, for instance, one can order any size, any dyes and any patterns one likes. And one can still buy wonderful qualities with more than 650 knots per square inch (1,000,000 per square metre) and made with the best wool in the world.

Among the nomads and in the villages, rugs are still being made in the traditional patterns and colours. These weavers aim at producing rugs as good as those made by their ancestors more than a thousand years ago, using the same simple tools. Here one still finds tradition and a feeling for dyes and patterns.

Finally, it must be emphasized that all true oriental rugs are always knotted by hand; all talk of mechanical production is simply slander. This handicraft is too valuable to the Orient to be spoiled.

The materials in an oriental rug are chiefly wool or silk combined with cotton. Flax and jute are used to a small extent only.

The pile is of wool, goats' hair and camel hair or silk. The warp may be of wool, cattle hair—or a mixture of the two, cotton, silk, flax and, in India, jute as well. The weft is made from the same materials as the warp.

Wool. The Persian lamb is widely known for its excellent wool. But even so, the quality varies considerably for several reasons. Climate and pasturage are two, since sheep from the hill regions, where the climate is colder, have a more pliable and stronger wool than those from warmer places near sea level. Moreover, not only does wool from different sheep vary in quality but there is a considerable difference between the wool from different parts of the same sheep. The wool of the Persian lamb is particularly suitable for rug making. It gives a mixture of rather coarse, long and glossy outer hair and finer, shorter and softer undercoat. The outer hairs give the material the necessary strength and glossiness, while the undercoat is necessary for spinning. Wool with a high proportion of soft, fine undercoat is most suitable for clothes but not at all for rugs. These require a coarser wool that gives a pile which is springy, dense, robust and glossy, i.e., a wool with a preponderance of long outer hairs. The weft, on the other hand, does not require the high glossiness. Nor does the material need to be so robust, since it is held by the warp. Consequently the weft can be made from a coarse, relatively short wool of a quality inferior to that used for the pile. The best wool in Persia comes from Kurdistan in the west and from Khurasan in the north-east. The sheep are generally sheared once a year, but sometimes twice. A particularly fine mixture is obtained by mixing the spring wool with lambs' wool, i.e., the wool obtained in the autumn from lambs born that spring. This mixture is used only for the very finest rugs.

Naturally there are comparable wools to be found in other countries of the East. Turkey, the Caucasus, Turkestan, India and China all produce wool fully equal to that from Persia.

Goat's hair (cattle hair) is not used to any great extent for the pile but mostly for warp and weft as well as for edging the sides of the rug. Camel hair is now used very seldom. The Camel-hair browns, e.g., in the Hamadan rugs, are generally dyed wool.

Camel hair has the unfortunate property of giving off a far from pleasant smell in hot, humid weather.

Silk is produced in the district round the Caspian Sea, where the climate is subtropical, and of course in China and Turkey. It is used for pile, warp and weft in the manufacture of exclusive, tightly woven rugs.

Artificial silk has also been introduced in recent times. However, this material is not as durable as pure silk and its appearance deteriorates when it becomes soiled and has to be washed.

Cotton is cultivated almost everywhere in Persia nowadays and spinning-factories are to be found in Tabriz, Kazvin, Isfahan, Yezd, Kashan and elsewhere. It is mostly used for warp and weft.

Flax is not particularly common in the warp and weft of oriental rugs. In Turkestan, India and sometimes even in Persia one finds rugs with the warp in this material, though these are usually particularly tightly woven rugs which need a thin warp.

Jute used to be used for the warp of Indian rugs, though not to any large extent. The material, which is hard and brittle, is not very durable.

The yarn is spun by hand with ancient, primitive tools.

After shearing, the wool is cleaned and sorted into different qualities according to use. It is then washed in streams or other watercourses, dried and bleached in the open air. After this treatment, it is sent to be carded. The nomads and some villagers, however, still card the wool by hand, using ancient methods.

The yarn is then spun by hand into different sizes according to use: the warp requires a yarn that is tightly and finely spun; the weft both coarse and fine yarn but not so tightly spun, and the pile a strong but quite loose yarn so that the ends of the knots have the appearance of brushes after they have been tied.

There are very few places in Persia where machine-spun yarn is used. In China, on the other hand, all rugs are now made from machine-spun yarn.

Cotton yarn is mostly spun by machine but sometimes by hand in simple rugs, if the manufacturer cannot afford to have the yarn spun or is prevented by transport difficulties.

Tanners' wool is a simpler and cheaper type of wool obtained from slaughtered animals. It is not cut from the hide but is loosened by a chemical process, which naturally affects its quality. This "dead" wool is never comparable with that from living animals; it is less durable, the dye does not take so well and the colours soon turn lifeless and shabby. The use of this type of wool is practically entirely confined to simple bazaar qualities.

The treatment of the wool involves so many important processes that it is worth mentioning a few details.

Before the sheep is sheared, it is usually washed if this is at all feasible. This gives two advantages: the wool will be cleaner and the animal is easier to shear. The wool is collected in bunches and immediately washed in running water. This should be done with great caution as the wool should remain greasy. It is then spread out on the ground to dry in the sun. It is turned continuously in order to get it dry as soon as possible and then it is sorted.

The dark and light wools are separated in sorting, since their use is always distinct and they are thus treated differently right from the start. Twigs and straw, which are always found, are also removed.

Carding is nowadays mostly done mechanically. But in the villages and among the nomads the ancient methods are still in use. Large quantities are beaten with a bow-like instrument, with the bowstring drawn very tight.

Hand spinning is done according to one of two methods, either by use of the spinning wheel and distaff, or of a heavy, almost pear-shaped wooden top, which requires great skill and gives a surprisingly even and fine yarn.

NATURAL DYES

In the Orient practically every family has had its own recipe for the dyeing of yarn in the various colours and these recipes have been handed down from generation to generation. They are based on animal and plant dyes and are naturally the best. They give the yarn a natural sheen.

A few examples of the most common plant dyes are given below:

Blue	indigo
Red	madder root, kermes and cochineal (dried scale insects)
Yellow	vine leaves, pomegranate peel, saffron
Brown	walnut shell, oak bark
Green	indigo+vine leaves or pomegranate peel
Black	indigo+henna, iron oxide (vinegar and iron filings)
Orange	henna+madder
Cream	walnut shell, pomegranate

In addition to the above there are innumerable mixtures and variations for deep and light shades, as well as many different ways of preparing the yarn for dyeing. Dyeing with a certain colour may take one day in one place, while the same colour some-where else and with some other method may take up to three or four days. Dyeing with indigo according to ancient methods may take no less than fifteen days.

ANILINE DYES

Since natural dyes require a time-consuming and laborious process it was not surprising that people succumbed to the temptation of using aniline dyes wherever possible, but the result did not come up to expectations. The Persian authorities gradually realized the danger to their foremost handicraft and, as already mentioned, introduced laws to hinder the use of aniline dyes. Their import was forbidden but even so they were smuggled into the country in large quantities and it proved difficult to keep a check on the dyers and rug manufacturers. In spite of all prohibitions and high export tariffs, a great many rugs were produced with aniline-dyed yarns.

The disadvantage with aniline dyes—apart from the fact that they fade and run—is that the wool loses its fat and becomes stiff and dry. Consequently, the fibres break more easily under pressure, which is bound to happen with a carpet.

Yarn coloured with vegetable dyes has exactly the opposite properties; the wool becomes softer and, moreover, retains the animal fat.

CHECKING THE DYE

How can the layman tell whether the yarn has been coloured with aniline or vegetable dye? A definite answer really requires a chemical analysis but here are some tips about how to detect anomalies that are characteristic of aniline-dyed yarn, provided that the carpet has been in use for some years or has been washed with alkaline substances.

Fold the carpet so that the pile separates right down the warp. With a vegetable dye, the yarn should be the same colour at the top of the pile as at the bottom, possibly with a slight difference in shade. On the other hand, if the difference in colour is great, e.g., blue-violet near the warp and blue-grey on the surface, or dark green near the warp and yellowish on the surface, one can be fairly certain that an inferior type of dye has been used, probably aniline.

With a completely new carpet that has not been washed with alkalis there will be no difference in colour; instead, inspect the parts of the carpet where uncoloured yarn borders with coloured. If the coloured dye has run on to the white area, an inferior dye has been used, though this discoloration may also be due to badly dyed weft yarn. It so happens that the weft of many types of carpet is dyed blue or red and since in general it is loosely woven and the dyer does not always use the best dyes for the warp and weft, the colours may run rather badly in the light parts of the carpet.

Another method is to dip a piece of white cloth in a strong soap solution and then rub it across the colours. If a lot of colour comes off on to the cloth, genuine dyes have not been used for that carpet. However, one must remember that yarn coloured with vegetable dyes may also give off some of its colour, though to a much slighter extent.

Even vegetable dyes can give a carpet a rather hard colour composition. In order to soften this effect and, above all, to improve the sheen, carpets are sometimes washed with various chemicals by specialists, usually with good results, but this method should not be attempted by a layman. On inspection, the pile of such a carpet will be found to be paler (bleached) at the top. A blue may be lighter at the surface but is nonetheless blue. Certain composite colours may have changed, e.g., a green may lose its yellow and become more blue at the surface. This latter case shows that the green has been dyed by using indigo+vine leaves or pomegranate peel.

The most beautiful changes in colour or shades come with age, which gives a slightly softer appearance and often heightens the sheen.

MODERN CHEMICAL DYES

Early in the present century much better synthetic dyes were introduced, which include the so-called alizarin and the advanced chrome dyes. In quality and fastness they are now almost equal with the vegetable dyes, with one tiny "but": the chemical dyes do not give the same warmth and softness as the vegetable dyes; instead, the carpet has a harder almost metallic sheen. This does soften, however, after about ten or fifteen years. Moreover, the dyes are fast to sunlight and washing, and experts hold that alizarin red and alizarin blue are fully comparable to the corresponding vegetable dyes, since they contain the same chemical substances.

CHARACTERISTIC COLOURS

The various carpet districts and countries have largely the following typical colours:

Turkestan, Hamadan, Seraband and Heriz: madder-lake.
Turkey, Meshed and Birjand: cochineal red.
The Caucasus, China and nomads: blue.
Kerman, Qum, Isfahan and Nain: cream or white.
Arak (Sultanabad): pink.

Many large districts, Tabriz among them, do not make particular use of any one colour.

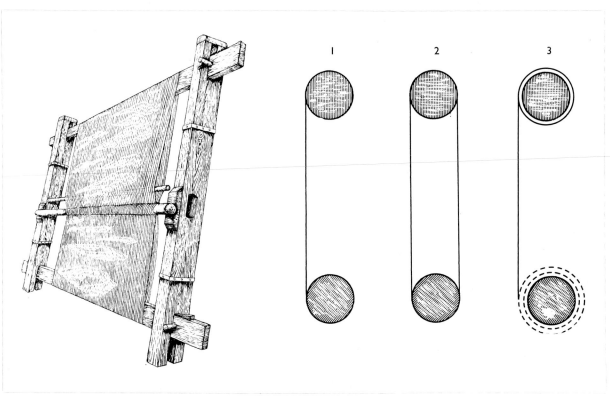

1. The ordinary type of loom has both the upper and the lower beam fixed.

2. Tabriz type. The lower beam can be removed.

3. Kerman type (roller beam type). Both beams can revolve and are fitted with ratchets. The warp is first wound round the upper beam and, as work progresses, the completed part of the rug is wound on to the lower beam.

Tabriz type loom and diagrams showing the warping on different types of loom.

There are four different types of loom, three upright and one horizontal. Timber that is sufficiently stout for the looms is hard to come by and the design of some of them may be rather weak as a result. The resultant carpets may have uneven edges or refuse to lie flat, due to the cross-beam having given way during weaving as a result of the weight of the carpet or the tension of the warp. Nowadays, looms are reinforced with iron fittings and such defects are less frequent. One cannot, however, expect that everything will be straight and true; a hand-woven carpet is bound to look different from one produced on a mechanical loom.

The four types of loom are:

1. *The ordinary upright type* which has the warp held between the upper and the lower beams. With this type one can weave a carpet that is as long as the distance between the beams. As work progresses, the weavers gradually raise the plank on which they sit.

2. *The Tabriz type (upright)*. Here the warp passes round both beams so that it runs down the front and the back of the loom. The lower beam can be slackened or tightened with the help of wooden wedges. With this type of loom carpets can be made

that are twice as long as the distance between the beams. The weavers do not have to raise their seat, since the lower beam can be slackened and the woven part of the carpet slid down and behind the loom. This type of loom is used throughout north-west and central Persia.

3. *Kerman and roller-beam type (upright)*. With this type of loom, the requisite length of warp yarn is wound on to the upper beam and the ends are attached to the lower beam. Both beams can be rotated and locked in position. As the weaving proceeds, the finished part of the carpet is rolled on to the lower beam. Carpets up to thirty or forty feet (around twelve metres) long can be produced with this type of loom. Such lengths cannot be achieved with the other two types already mentioned. Greater tension can be produced in the warp threads and consequently the carpets are even and straight.

4. *Nomad type (horizontal)*. Here the warp is simply stretched between two strong beams pegged to the ground. Since the nomads are continuously on the move to new pastures, they require a loom that is easy to set up and equally easy to dismantle and transport to their next settlement. As a result, their carpets are small and narrow. It is a curious sight to see them set up a warp about three feet (nearly one

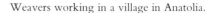
Weavers working in a village in Anatolia.

metre) wide but as much as fifteen feet (over four and a half metres) long, on which they weave three or four small carpets in a row.

There is, in fact, another horizontal type of loom in use. This is found in the modernized production of carpets in the Caucasus and in some parts of Turkestan.

Tools used in weaving a rug. (1) Shears for trimming the pile. (2) Steel comb for combing out the pile before trimming. (3) Hooked knife; the warp thread is caught with the hook and the yarn is then cut each time a knot is tied. (4) Old-type heavy iron comb. (5) Later, lighter iron comb. Both these iron combs are used for beating in the wefts.

As has already been stated, carpets are today woven in the Orient in exactly the same way as they were a thousand years ago. When people say that these carpets must be produced by mechanical means, they are speaking out of ignorance; presumably they cannot imagine that so even a carpet can be produced by hand. One reason for this attitude is probably that industrial products such as Wilton and Axminster carpets copy oriental patterns. Many people cannot see the difference between these and the genuine hand-woven carpet. Some oriental carpets cost so little that many people regard this as sufficient evidence that they cannot be hand-made. Anyone who has travelled in the East and seen a carpet being woven can, however, testify otherwise.

The weaver's instruments are simple and home-made. The yarn is cut off with a knife after the knot has been made. In Tabriz a knife fitted with a hook is used for catching up the warp threads. The weft and rows of knots are packed together with a heavy iron comb-beater with a handle. The newly woven part is combed with a strong steel comb before it is trimmed roughly while it is still in the loom. After the carpet has been removed from the loom it is given a final trim with shears and a razor-like instrument.

KNOTS

There are two basic knots, the Turkish *Ghiordes knot*, also known as the turkbaff, and the Persian *Sehna knot*, also known as the farsibaff.

The difference between them is that the Ghiordes knot encircles both warp threads, while the Sehna knot encircles one but is only loosely wound round the other. The difference is clearly shown in the drawings on the next page.

Each technique has its own advantages. Ghiordes is easier to tie in a coarse carpet, while Sehna gives a more elegant surface and better definition of the pattern.

A knot tied around one warp thread was used in Spanish carpets of the 15th-17th centuries, but is not found in the East.

The deceptive Jufti or "double knot", whereby the yarn is tied to four warp threads instead of two was first introduced in north-east Persia and parts of Turkestan. Unfortunately, this technique has spread rather rapidly. The great disadvantage is that the carpets do not wear so well, while some of the cheaper qualities lack density in the pile.

For the weaver, however, this technique doubles output as only half the number of knots have to be tied compared with the traditional method. The technique cuts cost but produces an inferior carpet.

Ghiordes knot
The two drawings on the left show how the knot is tied and its finished appearance. In the middle, three knots each round two warp threads; right, the Ghiordes knot round one and round four warp threads.

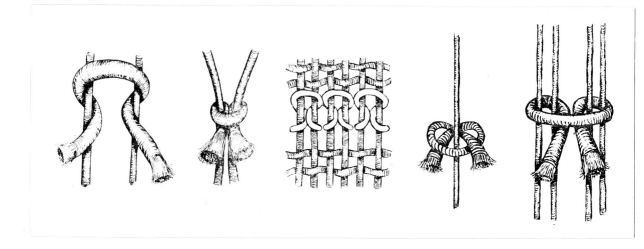

To tell whether a carpet has been knotted with the Ghiordes or the Sehna knot, fold it backwards and inspect the base of the pile. The top of the Ghiordes knot can be seen going across two warp threads. The ends of the knot emerge between the two warp threads under the top of the knot to form a bushy pile. The rows of Ghiordes knots, one above the other, form a pronounced stripe. The top of the Sehna knot only covers one warp thread, so that one end of the pile emerges immediately below it and the other on the far side of the second warp thread used for the knot. The second warp thread can usually be seen by separating the ends of the pile. In most cases the type of knot can be recognized simply by feeling the pile. A carpet woven with the Ghiordes knot usually has the nap running directly towards one end, while a carpet tied with the Sehna knot will have the nap running towards one corner.

The choice of knot varies a great deal between different districts, and both types are sometimes used in one and the same locality. The main reason for this is that people from different tribes have retained their traditional technique. The Turks use the Turkish knot and the Persians the Persian, but intermarriage and migration can lead to both knots being used within the same community.

In Persia and Turkey weaving is done by men, women and children. In the Caucasus, Turkestan and among the nomads, however, only the women weave. In China, India and Pakistan it is the men who sit at the looms, while women and children do the trimming, finishing off and other details. Output naturally varies from weaver to weaver, but is approximately 6,000–12,000 knots per 8-hour shift.

The usual method of producing a carpet is as follows. A certain number of warp threads are attached to the beam, according to the width and density required in the finished carpet. A simple mechanism separates alternate warp threads into two sets, creating an alley called the shed through which the weft is passed. The position of the two sets is reversed after the passage of each weft thread.

Before starting with the carpet proper, an edge or border of varying width is first woven, sometimes with a pattern, sometimes in different coloured bands.

When this has been done, knotting can begin. With the left hand or with the hooked knife, which is held throughout in the right hand, the weaver

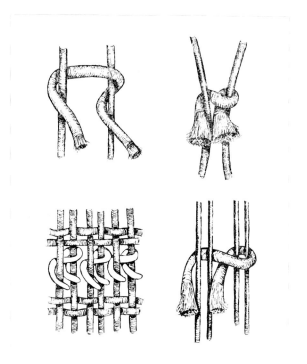

grasps two warp threads and ties a knot round these with both hands and pulls downwards, after which the yarn is cut.

After each row of knots, a weft thread is passed in between the warp threads above the row. Usually, two weft threads are passed between each row of knots. Kerman and Bijar carpets, however, have the weft in sets of three, while sets of four to six are found in carpets from Khurasan and Kazak as well as in the Samarkand, Khotan, Kashgar, and Yarkand carpets of East Turkestan. These larger sets produce a lateral ribbed pattern on the back of the carpet. In some cases a larger set of weft threads is included only after every fourth or sixth row of knots.

Sehna, Hamadan, Karaja and some of the Bahktiari carpets have only one weft thread between each row of knots. This technique is also discernible from the reverse of the carpet, where the warp threads are visible every other time they are left uncovered by the weft, producing a dotted appearance on the back. Another variation is to use what is known as a double warp. Here, one weft thread is passed between the warp threads at the usual tension but the next weft thread is inserted more loosely.

As a result, one of the warp threads will lie behind or under the other one, and the knot will lie on its side, thus increasing the carpet's density.

The row of knots and the wefts are now beaten together, using a heavy iron comb. This operation is repeated after every row of knots. After every third to fifth row comes the first rough trimming of the carpet, but the final trimming is not done until the carpet has been taken down from the loom. The work continues in this way until the carpet proper is finished, whereupon a second edge is woven, similar to that made at the beginning.

The sides or selvages of a carpet always have a protective edging, either woven in with the ordinary weft or oversewn after the process of weaving. The nomads ornament the sides of their carpets with tassels, and the ends are often in different colours.

Most carpets have fringes at both ends, but many from western Persia have a fringe at only one end, the other being simply the woven edge where knotting began. A fringe may be knotted or simply hang straight from the woven edge. Note that the end sewing, fringes and woven edges of carpets are frequently distinctive to certain districts, and so are of value in classification.

27

The enormous variety displayed by the designs of oriental carpets is a fascinating and stimulating study in itself. Different types of patterns and designs have been developed in different districts. Geometrical designs are often found together with other motifs but in some places they have been refined and may characterize the place of manufacture. The most common designs are those based on flowers but these have been revised and stylized into a number of different types. Religion is of decisive importance in the use of the human form in art. The Koran does not permit the portrayal of living beings. Both people and animals are portrayed nevertheless in Persia, where religious attitudes are more liberal, and in the Caucasus. This is also the case in China, where the designs are markedly different from those of Central Asia.

When considering the designs on different carpets one should bear in mind both the function of the carpet and the environment in which it was produced. A number of terms for carpets indicate their use, e.g., Enessi which indicates a door drapery, Hehbelyk which is a saddle cover and Namaslyk which is the prayer-rug of the Moslem. These terms also give some indication of the size. This is even more true of names like Ghali, which means carpet and stands for the large rectangular type usually found in the centre of a Persian room. Around this lie the Kenareher, runners, often comprising a series with the same design. There are several other similar terms, all of them with definite types of design suitable to their function and size (see pages 213-214).

So far as the conditions under which they are produced are concerned, a distinction must be made between carpets for domestic needs and those done to order on a more magnificent scale. The carpets produced by nomadic tribes differ from those made by the settled population in that they are woven more intuitively without recourse to any pattern or drawing. They are generally relatively small, with geometrical and stylized designs. Settled weavers usually work from a pre-designed pattern or cartoon and are thus able to produce carpets with richer, more varied designs. The cartoon is known as a Talim and consists of squared paper on which the pattern is reproduced. Each square stands for a knot in that particular colour. Mostly, the weavers work independently with this sketch in front of them. In the past, however, a

Drawing a cartoon.

Detail of cartoon, Talim. Above, part of the centre of the rug; below, the border.

Medallion rug (Persian).

foreman dictated the colours, particularly if two identical carpets were to be made. He then placed himself between a pair of looms and dictated the work for both carpets.

The composition of the design thus depends upon the type of carpet and follows carefully defined rules. On the basis of the pattern of the field, one can distinguish between four different types.

1. Medallion design.
2. All-over or repeat design.
3. Design with figures or representational design.
4. Niche and tree design.

The first group comprises the patterns in which the field, in a single colour or with small designs, is dominated by a central medallion. The second group, with its dense repeating pattern cut off by the borders, has a more ancient appearance and is often based on more geometrical shapes. The third group comprises the naturalistic reproductions of people and animals. The last group, the niche and tree design, is uniform from the point of view of

function, even though the pattern varies considerably.

These typical field designs are nearly always surrounded by a main border and narrower secondary borders or guards. Exceptions to this rule are, for instance, certain prayer rugs with the niche design and recent Saruk and Kerman carpets, which often have a broken floral border, and the Chinese carpets, which include a number of special types outside this classification.

The numerous details found in oriental carpets include a number that are very common. One of these is the Mir-Ibotha design, an oval figure filled with rosettes and flowers. This may be interpreted in several ways: as a winding river, as the imprint of a clenched, bloody hand, or as a flame. Another classical design, common as the main pattern, is the Shah Abbas design. This consists of large floral designs, cloud bands, arabesques, vases and palmettes (see illustration on page 31). Guli Henna is a pattern showing a stylized Henna plant. The Mina-Khani pattern, a floral design surrounded by four similar smaller flowers, is also used as a main design.

All-over "Shah Abbas" design (Persian).

Carpet with figures (Persian).

Turkish prayer rug.

Caucasian prayer rug.

Turkoman prayer rug with tree design (Baluchistan).

Persian prayer rug (below).

In the borders one finds patterns that are more familiar to the western world. A couple of examples of simple geometrical designs and ornaments are the meander (page 44) and the device called "the running dog" (page 39). The Greek cross is also found, but more common is the swastika, a symbol of happiness.

Another type of pattern sometimes found on carpets consists of inscriptions and dates with Arabic writing. The decorative inscriptions comprise aphorisms by some well-known author, such as Saadi, Hafez or Firdausi, but they may also be verses from the Koran. They are generally surrounded by a cartouche.

Dates in Arabic numerals refer, of course, to the Mohammedan calendar. This starts with Mohammed's journey from Mecca on the 16th July, 622 A.D. The Mohammedan year is shorter than ours by approximately 1/33. To arrive at a carpet's age on the basis of an Arabic date, e.g., 1322, proceed as follows:

Divide the date by 33 ($1322 \div 33 = 40$).
Subtract the quotient from the year ($1322 - 40 = 1282$).
Add 622 ($1282 + 622 = 1904$).

Thus a carpet of 1322 by the Arabic calendar should be dated 1904 according to our calendar.

However, one cannot always rely on a carpet's date being genuine. It has happened that the figures have been altered to a more advantageous date.

In the past each district used its traditional patterns and designs, which served as a means of telling where a particular carpet had been made. This is no longer the case; Tabriz patterns are now made in Kerman, and, vice versa, Seraband patterns in Turkey, Kerman patterns in Arak, etc.

Moreover, patterns strongly influenced by European taste are being used to a considerable extent. Thus, almost the entire production of Kerman is now concentrated on making carpets with floral patterns in the European style, with decorative medallions and broken floral borders, in order to satisfy buyers from Europe and other parts of the world. Carpets with European patterns and also intended for export are made in other districts as well.

This foreign element in the traditional patterns is naturally unfortunate and the native art is being threatened by new compositions. In some places and districts, however, this danger has been recognized and efforts are being made to restore the ancient patterns and at the same time abandon the modern thickness of certain carpets.

TURKEY

In Turkey carpets had been manufactured both for the domestic market and for export to Europe for centuries, but in about 1860 as a result of increased trade with Europe, manufacture was arranged in a more business-like manner and consequently the traditional patterns which had been associated with definite districts began to loose their identity. Prayer rugs are characteristic products of the old order. Their pattern and colour vary according to the place where they were made. The Turkish designs consist of geometrical forms and stylized floral patterns. As already mentioned, the portrayal of people and animals is prohibited, though in Kayseri and Brusa a number of hunting carpets have been produced in recent years, i.e., carpets portraying both people and animals.

Palmette diamond and smaller diamond design.

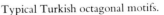

Typical Turkish octagonal motifs.

Border with tulip and rosettes.

Carnation border.

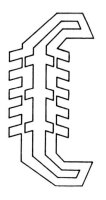

Stylized leaf design.

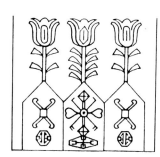

Design which, when placed directly under the prayer niche, is typical of Ladik rugs.

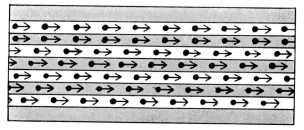

The special Kula border, which may comprise up to 12 parallel strips. This border is also found on Ghiordes rugs.

"Siebenbürger" border.

35

PERSIA

There is an enormous wealth and variety of patterns in Persian production. The geometrical patterns—cross, star and rosette designs—gave way in the 16th century to another type consisting of medallions, flowering tendrils and arabesques. There was also a tendency to allow the field to dominate the carpet's pattern.

The details are largely based on naturalistic floral patterns, though geometrical shapes also appear. The Persian craftsmen also depicted people and animals, indicating the perspective by placing the figures above instead of behind one another.

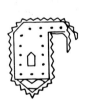

Persian floral and leaf designs, palmettes and an arabesque.

Different versions of the Mir-Ibotha design from Seraband, Hamadan and Sehna.

36

Mina-Khani design, a repeating pattern found in many variations.

Two plant motifs: the pomegranate and Guli Henna.

Cloud band, a Chinese pattern.

The Herati pattern, also known as the Mahi pattern (Mahi = fish), occurs with and without diamonds.

Left, two tree patterns, the tree of life and the weeping willow; right, a vase and tree pattern and a vase pattern.

Above downwards: Cloud band border, arabesque border, cartouche border, Herati border and Schekeri border.

THE CAUCASUS

The Caucasian types of carpet comprise both prayer rugs and carpets with a medallion design and repeating patterns. When the design is based on a large motif, smaller devices are often used to fill in the space. The patterns are essentially geometrical. Even flowers and figures, when used, are highly stylized.

Figures of man and woman showing the same stylized form.

Caucasian Mir-Ibotha design.

Stylized animals: dogs, camels and a bird.

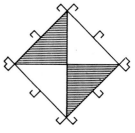

The hooked diamond is a stylized tarantula spider. The same design also occurs on some Central Asian rugs.

Two star motifs.

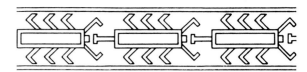

Scorpion border.

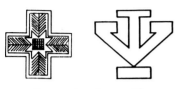

Cross and anchor motifs.

Crab-pattern border.

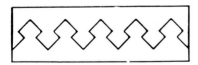

Perebedil motif.

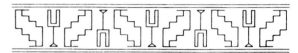

Border of wine glass and oak leaf.

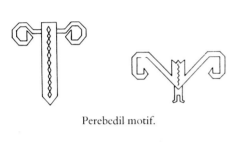

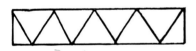

Georgian border. The name comes from Georgia in Trans-Caucasia.

Stylized rosette border.

Four border motifs: zig-zag motif, reciprocal motif, running dog and S-pattern.

Shirvan border.

39

TURKESTAN

The Turkoman carpets derive their character from being produced by a nomadic people. The carpets were woven for use in the Kibitkan, the tent. Only in recent times have carpets been made for sale; these are often different in size from those made for home use. The various tribes have their characteristic patterns, though geometrical diamonds and octagons dominate.

The Salors were once one of the most powerful peoples in Turkestan. Salor Gul is regarded as an original form of the Gul design.

Three types of Afghan octagon:

Turkoman rugs are largely based on geometrical octagon motifs, "Guls". The Guls of the Afghan district, also known as the elephant's foot, often vary in size and are placed as repeating patterns, often very close together.

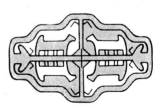

The Saryk octagon with its typical dogs, also found on Ersari rugs.

40

Turkoman hooked diamonds.

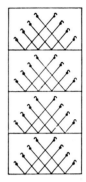

Design found on Enessi—draperies for covering Turkoman tent doors. A commercial term used for these draperies is Hatchlou.

Yomud Gul with linear anchor design in the field of the pattern.

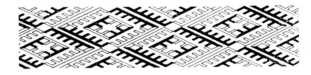

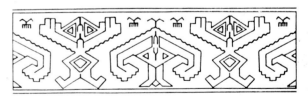

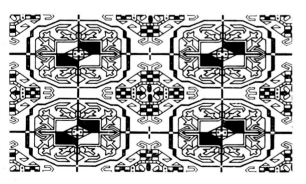

Tekke guls.

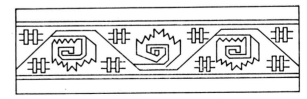

Border patterns typical of Turkestan: double-T border, hooked diamond border, Kabyrga or Avadan border and a stylized floral border.

41

Shou with swastika, round Shou and oblong Shou.

Three swastikas and a pattern built up from this motif.

CHINA

The patterns of Chinese carpets differ considerably from those of Central Asia. This is because the art of carpet-making came to China relatively late, probably in the 15th-17th centuries (if one excepts the few pieces said to have been produced around the 1st century A.D.). The patterns then adopted for carpets were taken from the other arts.

There are several special types of Chinese carpet: the temple carpet consists of two or more square fields with the same pattern; the pillar carpet has a human figure or a dragon covering the entire field and was intended to be wrapped around a pillar. The design is meant to join at the sides, thus it has no borders. The picture carpet, as its name suggests, is intended to be seen from one end only.

The patterns of the carpets are often symbolic and refer to Chinese, Taoist or Buddhist traditions. The Chinese symbols include the dragon, which is the finest, and was originally the emperor's emblem, symbolizing a positive and beneficial force, and the very common sign for happiness, *shou*, which appears in various designs. The swastika is very common and symbolizes long life, the number ten thousand and the heart of Buddha. Taoist symbols include the crane, indicating long life, the phoenix for immortality and the deer for prosperity. Another common animal symbol, of Buddhist origin, is the lion, the guardian of the temple. Border patterns may be of a general type such as the meander and pearl borders, but they also include stylized mountains and waves.

Yang and Yin, symbolizing creation, the Endless Knot and a symbol for the elements.

Chinese motifs. Cloud band, wave design and rock design.

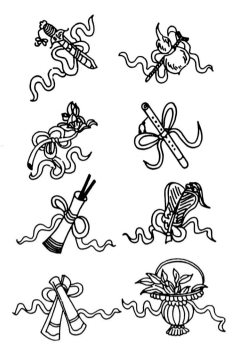

The patterns on Chinese carpets are often composed from certain groups of objects, e.g., the eight attributes of the Taoist immortal: the sword (imparts supernatural powers), the crutch (magic powers), the lotus flower (symbol of purity), the flute (brings happiness), magic rods (carried by the magician Chang), the sun clapper (can awaken the dead), the castanets (the stimulus of music) and the basket of flowers (conjures up sweet dreams).

The eight Buddhist symbols of happy augury: the baldachin (protects against all evil), the lotus flower (symbol of summer), the royal umbrella (royal dignity), the vase (lasting peace), the conch (calls to worship), the fishes (joy and sorrow or happiness and riches), the wheel of fire or the wheel of the law (divine justice) and the endless knot (eternity or long life).

Buddha's dog, Chih dsi, and Buddha's hand, a symbol of happiness.

The flowers of the four seasons: prunus (winter), tree peony (spring), lotus (summer) and chrysanthemum (autumn).

Chinese geometrical borders.

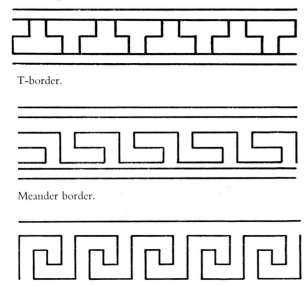

T-border.

Meander border.

Meander border.

Stylized floral border.

Naturalistic peony border.

Modern development of oriental rug and carpet-making has involved considerable rationalization of production methods, notably in the substitution of machine-spun for hand-spun yarns and the use of synthetic colouring. There has also been a movement to establish standard grades for the depth and density of pile.

Rationalization was made necessary largely because of rising costs, especially of labour. In those countries where rapidly improving economic and social conditions are giving much wider educational and career opportunities, it has become difficult to attract recruits to carpet-making, and considerably higher wages have now to be offered.

This situation is particularly acute in Persia, traditionally one of the major carpet-producing countries, but now transformed by the vast wealth derived from its oil exports. Although the government remains determined to promote the export of carpets, and subsidizes the industry, the greatly increased wages now necessary to attract an adequate labour force will drastically affect the final cost of the product. As a result, Persian hand-knotted carpets will face increasingly severe competition from those produced in less developed countries such as India and Pakistan, where good quality carpets, made by lower paid craftsmen, can still be manufactured and sold at considerably less cost. It remains to be seen whether, in these circumstances, Persian carpets can continue to dominate the world market.

In the mid-1970s the annual value of exported Persian carpets was around $100,000,000 to $120,000,000; of this, some $21,000,000-worth went to the United States and some £6,000,000-worth to the United Kingdom. During the years 1945 to 1965 export had been mainly of cheap quality examples of Hamadan, Shiraz, Karaja, Bahktiari, Tabriz and Kerman types. However, from the mid-1960s there has been increasing demand for better quality Isfahan, Nain, Keshan, Qum and Tabriz types, made with density grades as high as 650 knots per square inch, or about one million knots per square metre. It is satisfactory to note that, although the export market is still dominated by the cheaper varieties, production of high density carpets has increased during the last 20 years.

In Turkey there seems to have been no postwar increase in carpet-making, and those manufactured are still only small in size. Caucasian output remains low, although the industry is now state-controlled and production has marginally increased. The situation in Turkestan is similar, with a significant improvement in the quality of most of the Bokhara types produced. It is impossible even approximately to assess developments in China, although it seems likely that both the quality and the quantity of production has improved.

In India and Pakistan production and export of carpets, especially to Europe and the United States, has considerably increased. This success is largely due to a vast improvement in quality, both countries now producing close, tightly-knotted carpets with densities ranging from 160 to 390 knots per square inch or about 25 to 60 knots per square centimetre, and imitating Persian, Turkish and Turkoman designs. In the mid-1970s India exported approximately $15,000,000-worth of carpets annually to the United States and £1,200,000-worth to the United Kingdom; Pakistan's receipts were around $5,000,000 and £2,400,000 respectively.

The following description of oriental carpets is divided into six major groups in accordance with the largest producer countries. These will be treated in the following order:

TURKEY, PERSIA, THE CAUCASUS, TURKESTAN, CHINA, and INDIA and PAKISTAN.

This is followed by a section on woven carpets and Kelim.

The names of the many different carpets on the market indicate the place or district where they were made, or the name of the tribe which produced them.

There is always something to distinguish carpets of different districts. It may be the knot technique, the material, the colour, the pattern or the way in which the selvages are formed.

However, migration, intermarriage, and direct imitation of the techniques and patterns of other places may make it quite difficult for even a good expert to say where a carpet was produced and what its name should be. But anyone who has really become acquainted with the peculiarities of the various types should be able to do this ninety-five per cent of the time.

Another source of confusion is that the same name can be spelt in so many different ways. The English spelling used here is that which best indicates the Persian pronunciation of the different names.

The description of the major carpet districts includes some notes on historical, geographical and cultural circumstances that are of significance to the production of carpets.

Turkey

The carpet-producing places and districts of Turkey.

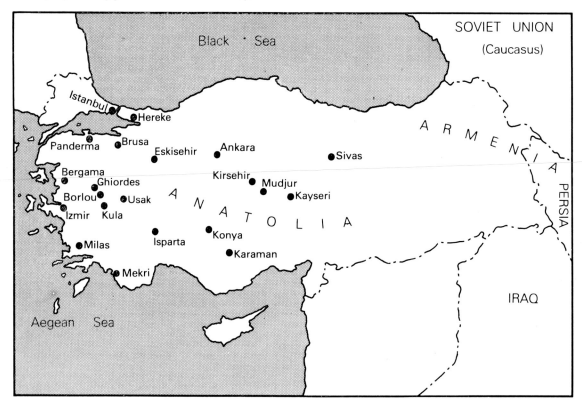

The oldest existing Turkish carpets are to be found in the city of Konya on the ancient trade route from Syria and Mesopotamia to Europe. They are considered to be from the 13th century, when the Seljuk dynasty was still in power in Asia Minor with Konya as the capital. Several mosques and burial chambers tell of the lively pilgrim city and commercial centre of that time. Having lain for centuries in the Ala-ed-din mosque, the carpets have now been removed to the temple of the Maulavier Order, which is now a museum for Seljuk and Osman art.

The craftsmen of Konya and the entire province have a traditional name for their masterly skill and the district is a centre for Turkish carpet-making. The place has been known for thousands of years. Monuments with a curious pictorial writing show that it was occupied by the Hittites, who ruled over much of Asia Minor from about 2100-1300 B.C. Konya (ancient Iconium) remained important for many centuries. Saint Paul suffered persecution there during his journeys through Asia Minor. Later it was the capital of the Roman province of Lycaonia, and from 1099 A.D. of the Seljuk sultanate of Rum.

Turkish carpet-making has been influenced to a considerable extent by the Greeks, who for centuries dominated production on the west coast of Anatolia and the islands off the mainland. It was chiefly the Greek communities that, together with the Armenians and the Kurds, took care of production in Turkey. The Greeks, however, were expelled when the republic was set up in 1923, and Turkey's population now consists of about 86 per cent of Turks. There is now no national religion but the Mohammedan creed is acknowledged by the great majority.

In the 16th and 17th centuries the standard of Turkish carpets was very high and the pieces from those times are fully equal to the carpets of Persia. The sultans imported Persian designers as well as extremely skilful dyers and weavers who were commissioned to produce magnificent articles for the court.

In the home, carpets were woven for domestic use, particular care being taken with the prayer rugs. Almost every home had one or two looms. Carpet-making was a traditional domestic craft particularly in Izmir (Smyrna), Ghiordes, Usak, Kula and Sivas. During the second part of the

49

Traditional types:	Kula	Ladik	Modern types:
Panderma	Ushak	Kayseri	Sparta
Milas	Kirsehir	Yuruk	Eskisher
Mekri	Konya	Hereke	Ghiordes
Ghiordes	Mudjur	Saff	Ushak
Bergama	Sivas		Borlou

19th century European trading houses started the mass production of large carpets of coarse quality with imitation Persian designs. With the introduction of aniline dyes for this commissioned work the vegetable dyes traditionally used in the East began to be abandoned. The art of carpet-making was in danger of being degraded.

Turkish carpets are very different in type from Persian. They are more coarsely woven and always with the Ghiordes knot. The patterns are different, being based more on prayer niches, and the designs are more geometrical. The Koran does not permit the portrayal of people and animals, though hunting scenes have appeared in recent years on carpets from Kayseri and Brusa. They are probably woven by Armenians.

Carpets from Asia Minor are collectively known as Anatolian. The varieties are named after their place of manufacture or the commercial centre where they are purchased for further transport. Thus a Smyrna carpet may have been woven in the interior —many come from the south-western province of Aydin. The largest producers are Ankara and the province of Konya. The older carpets from the city of Usak beyond Smyrna, an ancient seat of carpet-making, are easily recognized by their technique and exquisite colours.

However, it is not very convenient to describe the Turkish carpets on a geographical basis and consequently they have been grouped into older and modern types. The former group includes the carpets still being made today according to ancient methods without any European influence.

The latter, with each carpet noted as "modern production", are described at the end of the section.

52

Mekri   3 ft. 1 in. × 5 ft. 7. in. approx.
(95 × 170 cm.).
Main design: central panel divided in two, each half identical, with oblong panel enclosing a double floral design. Both ends have double niches. The light ground of the inner field has a faint pattern of colour shades. Main border: roughly stylized floral pattern. Made in the 1930s.

Milas   3 ft. 6 in. × 5 ft. 1 in. approx.
(107 × 154 cm.).
Main design: prayer niche with stepped and hooked Mihrab; above the niche a panel with design resembling candlesticks. Main border: star design; guards with same pattern. Made after 1920.

MILAS

Made in: Milas, south-east of Ismir (formerly Smyrna).
Knot: Ghiordes.
Warp: wool.
Weft: wool or cotton, with 2-4 shoots after each row of knots.
Pile: coarse wool.
Fringe: narrow woven, coloured edge and fringe at either end.
Design: prayer niche predominates, inner field no wider than the width of the borders, in other typical patterns the field is divided by longitudinal zig-zag design.
Colours: many shades of red.
Sizes: small carpets up to 4 ft. 5 in. × 6 ft. 11 in. approx. (135 × 210 cm.).
Density: 58-103 knots per sq. in. approx. (9-16 knots per sq. cm.).

MEKRI

Made in: Mekri, south-east of Milas.
Knot: Ghiordes.
Warp: wool.
Weft: wool, white or grey, 2 shoots after each row of knots.
Pile: coarse wool.
Fringe: usually two-coloured, woven edge and fringe at either end.
Design: stylized floral design in a divided field, one half red and the other blue, or with other contrasting colours, also zig-zag pattern.
Colours: red, yellow or beige.
Sizes: usually rugs, sometimes gallery size.
Density: 58-103 knots per sq. in. approx. (9-16 knots per sq. cm.).

54

Ghiordes   4 ft. 1 in. ×6 ft. approx.
                    (125 ×184 cm.).
Main design: a distinctive prayer niche with
pillars; panel frieze with floral pattern at
either end. Main border: flowers and
arabesque. Ghiordes carpets generally have
many borders. i.e., 7–15. Made around 1860.

Ghiordes   4 ft. 9 in. ×9 ft. approx.
                    (145 ×275 cm.).
Main design: medallion pattern with
corners that form a pointed Mihrab at either
end, with a panel frieze outside this. Main
border: comb-like leaf pattern and floral
pattern. Made around 1860.

GHIORDES

Made in: the city of Ghiordes, approximately 93
miles (150 km.) north-east of Izmir.
Knot: Ghiordes.
Warp: wool or cotton, sometimes silk.
Weft: cotton, 2 shoots after each row of knots.
Pile: fine quality wool, cut short, sometimes with
cotton for certain details.
Fringe: narrow woven edge and fringe at either end.
Design: mostly niche design with columns and
often a pendant or flower bouquet hanging from
the apex of the Mihrab, the point of the niche.
Usually one or two panel friezes above and below the field. A large number of borders. Another
version has a medallion with corners that form a
pointed Mihrab at either end. Borders with a
stylized comb-like leaf design.
Colours: Beige, blue, green, pink or red.
Sizes: small prayer rugs and up to 4 ft. 2 in. ×6 ft. 7 in.
approx. (130×200 cm.). Medallion carpets in sizes
up to 5 ft. 10 in. ×14 ft. 9 in. approx. (180×450 cm.).
Density: 77-226 knots per sq. in. approx. (12-35
knots per sq. cm.).

Bergama   5 ft. 1 in. × 5 ft. 11 in. approx.
(155 × 180 cm.).
Main design: two large octagons enclosing
two smaller ones plus star and cross designs.
Main border: hooked diamond pattern.
Made around 1850.

Kula   3 ft. 9 in. × 5 ft. 3 in. approx.
(115 × 162 cm.).
Main design: prayer niche with the green
inner field dominated by a distinctive floral
design. A panel frieze with floral pattern
above the point of the Mihrab niche. Main
border: stylized carnations. Outermost
guard, "alligator" border. Made at the end
of the 18th century.

BERGAMA

Made in: the town of Bergama, north of Izmir.
Knot: Ghiordes.
Warp: wool, usually dyed.
Weft: wool, usually dyed, 2-6 shoots after each row
of knots.
Pile: coarse quality wool.
Fringe: broad multicoloured woven edge with fringe
at either end.
Design: geometrical medallions and other designs
reminiscent of the Kazak carpets, with, e.g., wine
glass design in the borders.
Colours: red in shades of brown.
Sizes: many rather square rugs but up to 5 ft. 2 in. ×
8 ft. 10 in. approx. (160 × 270 cm.).
Density: 77-155 knots per sq. in. approx. (12-24
knots per sq. cm.).

Some of the older carpets appear to be made
in relief, owing to the fact that the yarn for the
basic colour is spun to the left and that for other
colours is spun to the right. After being used for
some time, the yarns lie in opposite directions,
giving a relief effect.

KULA

Made in: Kula, approximately 62 miles (100 km.)
south of Ghiordes.
Knot: Ghiordes.
Warp: wool, coarsely spun.
Weft: in older carpets wool, in newer carpets cotton,
with 2 shoots after each row of knots.
Pile: wool of a somewhat coarser type than in
Ghiordes carpets.
Fringe: narrow woven edge and fringe at either end.
Design: much the same as Ghiordes, though only
one panel as compared with the two-four in Ghiordes
carpets; moreover, instead of a pendant the Kula
carpet has one or two tendrils in the field. Either a
prayer niche or a double Mihrab at either end. The
typical Kula border consists of a large number of
narrow stripes in two contrasting colours, enclosing
a tiny flower design.
Colours: dark blue, red or yellow-brown and
occasionally green.
Sizes: mostly small and up to 4 ft. 8 in. × 6 ft. 11 in.
approx. (140 × 210 cm.).
Density: 58-161 knots per sq. in. approx. (9-25 knots
per sq. cm.).

58

Ushak 4 ft. 7 in. ×6 ft. 5 in. approx.
(140×195 cm.).
Main design: inner field with vase and floral pattern, with a Mihrab at either end. The corners have heavily stylized flowers and leaves. Main border: hooked carnation border. Made around 1910.

USHAK (old type)

Made in: the town of Usak near Ghiordes and Kula.
Knot: Ghiordes.
Warp: wool, dyed.
Weft: wool, dyed, 2 shoots after each row of knots.
Pile: fine quality wool.
Fringe: coloured woven edge and fringe at either end.
Design: large diamonds and star-shaped medallions, arabesques and curved designs almost in the Persian style, as well as vases with stylized floral design.
Colours: dark red or dark blue.
Sizes: mostly large, oblong and up to 8 ft. 2 in. × 14 ft. 9 in. approx. (250×550 cm.).
Density: 103-270 knots per sq. in. (16-42 knots per sq. cm.).

This old type is no longer made and the carpets that are still to be had are consequently extremely valuable. Densely knotted and with a short pile, they are unlike the ones made today, which are woven from coarse yarn and are consequently very thick. The new type is described later in this section.

Kirsehir 2 ft. 9 in. ×5 ft. 1 in. approx.
(85×155 cm.).
Main design: medallion with double Mihrab, panel friezes with floral pattern at either end. Main border: heavily stylized floral pattern. Made after 1945.

KIRSEHIR

Made in: the town of Kirsehir, south-east of Ankara.
Knot: Ghiordes.
Warp: wool, dyed.
Weft: wool, dyed, 2 shoots after each row of knots.
Pile: fine, somewhat stiff wool.
Fringe: narrow, coloured, woven edge with an ordinary or braided fringe at either end.

Design: niche design of two types, one with an empty field, the other with the field decorated with cypresses, a so-called grave carpet (Turbeh-lik) or with a mosque design. Another type has a medallion with a double Mihrab.
Colours: red.
Sizes: mostly rugs.
Density: 58-129 knots per sq. in. approx. (9-20 knots per sq. cm.).

59

Konya   2 ft. 3 in. ×3 ft. 7 in. approx. (68 × 110 cm.).

Main design: geometrical medallion with stepped corners, forming a double Mihrab. Main border: stylized carnations. The striking difference between the design at the end and that of the rest of the rug is typical of the Konya carpet. Made in the 1930s.

KONYA

Made in: the town of Konya, approximately 186 miles (300 km.) south of Ankara.

Knot: Ghiordes.

Warp: wool.

Weft: wool, 2 shoots after each row of knots.

Pile: coarse wool.

Fringe: narrow, coloured woven edge with fringe at either end.

Design: geometrical and zig-zag patterns in the older carpets. The newer ones have a niche design resembling Kirsehir and Mudjur. The panel frieze above the apex of the niche may be somewhat larger than these two types. Medallion patterns are also found.

Colours: yellow-beige or red.

Sizes: small and up to 4 ft. 7 in. ×7 ft. 1 in. approx. (140×215 cm.).

Density: 58-129 knots per sq. in. approx. (9-20 knots per sq. cm.).

Mudjur   3 ft. 6 in. ×4 ft. 9 in. approx. (106 × 144 cm.).

Main design: stepped prayer niche. The inner field is dominated by a double hooked diamond, there is a diagonal carnation design along the sides of the niche and a panel frieze above its point. Main border with stylized floral design. Made in the 1930s.

MUDJUR

Made in: Kirsehir district in central Anatolia.

Knot: Ghiordes.

Warp: wool.

Weft: wool, dyed, 2 shoots after each row of knots.

Pile: coarse wool.

Fringe: narrow, coloured woven edge and fringe at either end.

Design: niche design, so-called Mihrab; above the niche a patterned panel frieze.

Colours: cochineal red or madder red.

Sizes: rugs.

Density: 58-129 knots per sq. in. approx. (9-20 knots per sq. cm.).

Sivas 4 ft. 4 in. ×6 ft. 5 in. approx. (132 × 195 cm.).
Main design: geometrical rod medallion with stepped corners; the entire inner field covered with the Herati pattern. Main border: stylized floral and arabesque pattern. Made in the 1930s.

SIVAS

Made in: the town of Sivas and the neighbouring district in central eastern Anatolia.

Knot: Ghiordes.

Warp: finely spun cotton or wool.

Weft: cotton or wool, 2 shoots after each row of knots.

Pile: fine quality wool.

Fringe: narrow, woven edge with braided or ordinary fringe at either end.

Design: large six-pointed medallions or Persian hunting and medallion designs.

Colours: light beige, red, pink, yellow-gold or dull blue.

Sizes: the older pieces are mostly rugs, the newer ones are larger.

Density: 103-236 knots or more per sq. in. (16-35 knots per sq. cm.).

Kayseri   3 ft. 7 in. ×6 ft. approx.
(110 × 182 cm.).
Main design: an exact copy of a Ghiordes pattern, prayer niche, side pillars, pendant and the two panel friezes. Main border: flower and leaf design, the pattern reminiscent of the Herati border. Made after 1945.

KAYSERI

Made in: the town of Kayseri approximately 93 miles (150 km.) south-east of Kirsehir.
Knot: Ghiordes.
Warp: cotton or silk.
Weft: cotton or silk, two shoots after each row of knots.
Pile: fine quality wool or silk.
Fringe: narrow, woven edge and braided or ordinary fringe at either end.
Design: imitation Ghiordes or Persian designs of all types. When silk is used for the pile, the work is mostly rather coarse and the silk not of the very best quality.
Colours: red, blue, yellow-gold and beige.
Sizes: mostly rugs but up to 6 ft. 3 in. ×9 ft. 10 in. approx. (190 × 300 cm.).
Density: 77-236 knots per sq. in. approx. (12-35 knots or more per sq. cm.).

Ladik   3 ft. 4 in. × 5 ft. 11 in. approx.
(102 × 180 cm.).
Main design: prayer niche; under this three pentagonal motifs side by side with three tulip designs with long stalks. Main border with stylized floral design. Made around 1920.

LADIK

Made in: the town of Ladik north-west of Konya.
Knot: Ghiordes.
Warp: wool, dyed.
Weft: wool, dyed, with 2 shoots after each row of knots.
Pile: fine quality wool.
Fringe: narrow, coloured, woven edge and fringe at either end.

Design: niche design with empty field; below the base of the niche three pentagonal designs joined together, with from three to six tulip-like designs issuing from them on long stalks. The end borders are sometimes half as broad as those down the sides.
Colours: red.
Sizes: rugs.
Density: 58-161 knots per sq. in. approx. (9-25 knots per sq. cm.).

Yuruk   3 ft. 9 in. × 11 ft. 2 in. approx.
(115 × 340 cm.).
Main design: large star design in the Caucasian manner surrounded by stylized floral pattern. Main border: stylized floral pattern on light ground, surrounded by two borders with wavy floral pattern. Made in the 1930s.

YURUK

Made by: nomad tribes wandering in eastern Anatolia up towards the Sea of Marmara.
Knot: Ghiordes.
Warp: wool and goats' hair, brown or dyed.
Weft: wool and goats' hair, dyed, 2-4 shoots after each row of knots.
Pile: long coarse wool.
Fringe: pattern woven into edges with plaited fringes.
Design: geometrical design, resembling Kazak carpets, e.g., stars, swastika, spider, "S" design.
Colours: dark reddish, blue and brown.
Sizes: rugs and up to 4 ft. 11 in. × 9 ft. 2 in. approx. (150 × 280 cm.); also long narrow types.
Density: 58-129 knots per sq. in. approx. (9-20 knots per sq. cm.).

HEREKE

Made in: Hereke on the Sea of Marmara.
Knot: Ghiordes.
Warp: cotton or silk.
Weft: cotton or silk, 2 shoots after each row of knots.
Pile: fine quality wool or silk.
Fringe: woven edge and fringe at either end.
Design: apart from some patterns in the French style, copies are made of classical Persian designs.
Colours: red or beige.
Sizes: rugs and up to 4 ft. 11 in. × 7 ft. 6 in. approx. (150 × 230 cm.).
Density: 236-452 knots per sq. in. approx. (35-70 knots or more per sq. cm.).

Silk-Hereke   4 ft. × 5 ft. 5 in. approx.
(122 × 165 cm.).
Main design: discreet medallion pattern in the Persian style with corners, floral designs covering the entire inner field. Main border in the Herati pattern. Made at the turn of the century.

SAFF

Made in: the Kayseri and Brusa districts.
Knot: Ghiordes.
Warp: cotton or silk.
Weft: cotton, 2 shoots after each row of knots.
Pile: wool or silk.
Fringe: narrow, woven edge and fringe at either end.
Design: small prayer niches in different colours, placed side by side; they vary in number from 2-9. The Arabic word "saff" means a "row" and the popular name for these pieces is family prayer rug.
Colours: all.
Sizes: up to 3 ft. 7 in. × 10 ft. 10 in. approx. (110 × 330 cm.).
Density: 77-236 knots per sq. in. approx. (12-35 knots per sq. cm.).

Silk-Saff   2 ft. 9 in. × 7 ft. 6 in. approx. (85 × 230 cm.).
Main design: small prayer niches in various colours. Main border: carnation design. Small niches like those of the Konya rug at either end. Made after 1945.

Sparta   5 ft. 3 in. ×8 ft. 8 in. approx.
(160 ×265 cm.).
Main design: distinct Herati pattern. Main
border: geometrical, stylized floral pattern
in the Caucasian style. Made in the 1930s.

SPARTA   (modern production)

Made in: Isparta, west of Konya in southern Anatolia.
Knot: Ghiordes.
Warp: cotton, coarsely spun.
Weft: cotton, 2 shoots after each row of knots.
Pile: coarse wool.
Fringe: narrow, coloured woven edge with braided fringe at either end.
Design: the same as for Eskisher, Persian and Turkoman. The most popular patterns are Seraband and Tekke-Bokhara.
Colours: red, pink, blue or beige.
Sizes: mostly large carpets.
Density: 26-77 knots per sq. in. approx. (4-12 knots per sq. cm.).

Eskisher   6 ft. 8 in. ×8 ft. 2 in. approx.
(200 ×250 cm.).
Main design: copy of Persian medallion
pattern. Main border has floral pattern in
the Persian style. Made after 1945.

ESKISHER   (modern production)

Made in: Eskisehir, west of Ankara.
Knot: Ghiordes.
Warp: coarsely spun cotton.
Weft: coarsely spun cotton, 2 shoots after each row of knots.
Pile: heavy, coarsely spun wool.
Fringe: narrow, coloured, woven edge with braided fringe at either end.
Design: imitation Persian, Turkoman and Chinese patterns.
Colours: red, pink, blue or beige.
Sizes: mostly large carpets.
Density: 26-77 knots per sq. in. approx. (4-12 knots per sq. cm.).

GHIORDES (modern production)

Made in: Ghiordes and the Kula district.
Knot: Ghiordes.
Warp: wool or cotton.
Weft: wool or cotton, 2 shoots after each row of knots.
Pile: coarsely spun wool, sometimes also with cotton.
Fringe: narrow, woven edge and braided fringe at either end.
Design: all-over floral pattern or medallion design.
Colours: light pink, blue, green or beige.
Sizes: anything up to 9 ft. 10 in. ×13 ft. approx. (300×400 cm.).
Density: 26-39 knots per sq. in. approx. (4-6 knots per sq. cm.).

Ghiordes　　5 ft. 7 in. ×7 ft. 9 in. approx. (170×235 cm.).
Main design: medallion pattern resembling Tabriz. Main border: stylized flower and leaf border resembling the Herati. Made in the 1930s.

USHAK (modern production)

Made in: the town of Usak near Ghiordes and Kula.
Knot: Ghiordes, coarse and loosely tied.
Warp: wool dyed red or green.
Weft: wool, dyed, 2 shoots after each row of knots.
Pile: wool, coarse and loosely spun.
Fringe: narrow, coloured, woven edge and short fringe at either end.
Design: large, naturalistic leaf design, forming diamonds and medallions. The pattern is known as Yaprak after the town of Yapraklar, where a large number of these carpets are sold. Another pattern has a rectilinear medallion surrounded by an empty field.
Colours: a strong red, sometimes green or beige.
Sizes: mostly large carpets.
Density: 13-26 knots per sq. in. approx. (2-4 knots per sq. cm.).

Ushak   9 ft. 2 in. × 12 ft. 10 in. approx. (280 × 390 cm.).
Main design: Yaprak pattern comprising large diamonds with hooked design and large floral design. Main border: leaf and flower design. Made in the 1930s.

BORLOU (modern production)

Made in: Borlou, near Ghiordes in western Anatolia.
Knot: Ghiordes.
Warp: cotton, coarsely spun.
Weft: cotton, 2 shoots after each row of knots.
Pile: wool, coarsely spun and rather long.
Fringe: narrow, woven edge and fringe at either end.
Design: all-over floral design inside an empty field, otherwise like Eskisher.
Colours: beige, pink, blue and green in pastel shades.
Sizes: mostly large carpets.
Density: 26-39 knots per sq. in. approx. (4-6 knots per sq. cm.).

Borlou   8 ft. 2 in. × 11 ft. 10 in. approx. (250 × 360 cm.).
Main design: all-over floral design resembling the Persian Tabriz carpets. Main border: Herati-like floral border.

Persia

Regions and places in Persia where carpets are produced.

Azerbaijan:

Tabriz
Heriz
Georavan
Meriban
Karaja
Sarab
Bakshaish
Ardabil

Central area

Joshaghan
Saruk
Kashan
Bahktiari
Arak
Feraghan
Hamadan
Semnan
Teheran
Qum
Luristan (nomad)
Lilihan

Malayer
Kazvin
Nain
Seraband
Mahal
Isfahan

Kerman and Fars:

Kerman
Abadeh
Shiraz
Yezd
Afshar   (nomad)
Kashgai (nomad)

Khurasan:

Qain
Birjand
Turkbaff
Durukhsh
Khurasan
Meshed

Kurdistan:

Bijar
Zenjan
Sanandaj (Sehna)
Kermanshah
Kurdistan (nomad)

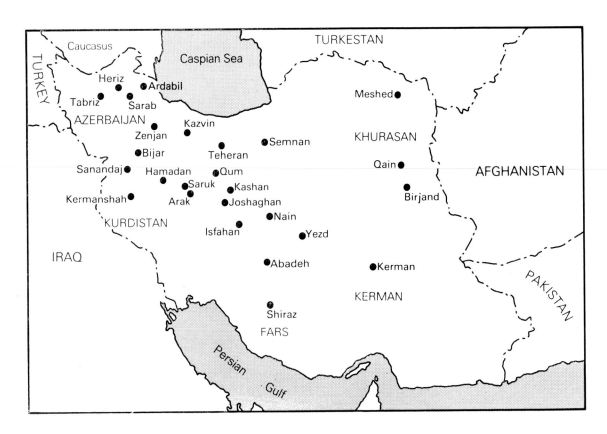

There is something about oriental works of art that reminds us of the fairy-tale atmosphere of the Arabian Nights. The Persian carpet with its enchantingly beautiful colours is no exception. The Persians proudly guard their heritage. Their carpet-weaving is the best in the world. For many centuries the Persian carpet has been second to none in originality, colour harmony and artistic execution.

Persia has an area about seven times that of Great Britain but only 5-10 per cent can be cultivated. Most of the country is mountainous, with the inner plain lying as much as 4,920 feet (1,500 metres) above sea level, crossed and hemmed in by high-ridged chains of mountains.

The official name of the country is now Iran, the ancient Persians' name for their country. The population is made up of numerous races and tribes. About half are Tajiks, descendants of the ancient Persians. The vast majority are Moslems and adherents of the Shi'a sect.

Agriculture is the main source of livelihood and requires co-operation between the nomads and the settled population. The nomads, who wander over the pastures in the mountains with their herds of goats and sheep, supply meat, hides and wool, butter and cheese. In the plains, where the dry climate generally makes irrigation essential, wheat, barley and rice are cultivated as well as tobacco, tea, fruit and grapes.

Carpets are made both by the nomadic herdsmen and by the settled Tajiks in the plain. The Turkish-speaking people mostly use the Ghiordes knot, the Persian-speaking the Sehna knot. The arts of weaving and dyeing are handed down from father to son, from mother to daughter. The girl who weaves the most beautiful carpet can be certain of having the most suitors.

Among the settled peoples, men, women and children take part in the work; among the nomads it is primarily the women who make the carpets—the men have their herds and hunting to think of.

The settled population weave carpets of all types and sizes, while the primitive looms of the nomads restrict them to the smaller pieces.

The prayer rug, on which the Moslem faces Mecca to say his prayers, is executed with particular care. It must be made of yarn in true colours, dyed with vegetable and animal dyes, as otherwise the prayers would remain unheard.

Many colours have a symbolic meaning:

Tabriz carpet with figures
7 ft. 10 in. × 11 ft. 2 in. approx.
(240 × 340 cm.).
Apart from the many animal designs, there are a number of biblical details in this carpet —King Solomon in the upper part, the child Moses in the centre. The border is made up of animal, human and cherub designs. Made in the early 1920s.

Green is sacred to the faithful. It is the Prophet's colour and is seldom found except in prayer rugs and other sacred carpets.

Red signifies sorrow for some Moslems and happiness for others.

Yellow indicates power and glory (for the ancient Egyptians, however, it signified sorrow).

When the aniline dyes started to invade the market, the Persian authorities recognized the danger to the quality of the carpets and prohibited their importation. The dyer found breaking this law had his workshop razed to the ground. He also lost his right hand.

Tabriz　　　　6 ft. 3 in. ×9 ft. 4 in. approx.
(190 × 285 cm.).
Main design: medallion design surrounded by lotus and Mina-Khani flowers as well as cloud band design. The main border has oval cartouches with writing resembling Kufic, as well as four circles with Arabic text. The innermost guard has large cartouches with Arabic writing, probably verses by some famous poet. The outermost guard has stalks of the henna flower and shows an unusual way of decorating the outer edge of a carpet. The pattern is taken from miniature painting of the 17th century. Made after 1945.

TABRIZ

Made in: Tabriz, provincial capital of Eastern Azerbaijan, approximately 390 miles (630 km.) from Teheran. 5,020 ft. (1,530 m.) above sea level.
Knot: Ghiordes or Sehna.
Warp: cotton.
Weft: cotton, 2 shoots after each row of knots.
Pile: coarse, somewhat rough wool trimmed short.
Fringe: narrow woven edge with ordinary or knotted fringe.
Design: medallion and corner design, all-over floral pattern, vase with figures, tree and hunting designs. Cartouches with inscriptions.
Colours: beige, red, pink or dark blue.
Sizes: all.
Density: 77-452 knots per sq. in. approx. (12-70 knots or more per sq. cm.).

Tabriz is the second largest city in Persia and one of the largest producers of carpets in the country. Manufacture is geared to exports and the quality varies considerably, from the simplest bazaar quality to the most luxurious pieces. Tabriz is the only carpet centre in the country where synthetic dyes predominate. A major problem is how to obtain soft colour composition in the medium qualities, since these are traditionally made up of bright contrasting colours.

The carpets of Tabriz are generally among the best in Persia. They have a characteristically stiff and short pile, which makes them easy to look after and practical for all purposes.

Georavan   7 ft. 9 in. × 10 ft. 5 in. approx.
(235 × 318 cm.).
Main design: roughly drawn rod medallion,
surrounded by stylized floral design, corners
in contrasting colour. Main border: roughly
stylized Herati border. Made after 1945.

Heriz   6 ft. 3 in. × 9 ft. 6 in. approx.
(190 × 290 cm.).
Main design: geometrical medallion and
stylized floral design, corners in contrasting
colour. Main border: highly stylized Herati
border. Made after 1945.

HERIZ

Made in: the village of Heriz approximately 40
miles (65 km.) north-east of Tabriz. 4,590 ft. (1,400
m.) above sea level.
Knot: Ghiordes.
Warp: cotton, coarsely spun.
Weft: cotton, coarsely spun, 2 shoots after each row
of knots.
Pile: heavy wool.
Fringe: narrow, woven edge with ordinary or
knotted fringe.
Design: geometrical medallion and corner designs,
also over-all pattern with large stylized leaf designs
and in a few cases a cypress design.
Colours: madder red, blue or beige.
Sizes: Mostly large but a few rugs.
Density: 58-236 knots per sq. in. approx. (9-35 knots
per sq. cm.).
    Generally a coarsely woven carpet but, even so,
very durable. Particularly suitable for a hall or
dining-room.

GEORAVAN

Made in: the village of Georavan near Heriz (Azer-
baijan). 4,790 ft. (1,460 m.) above sea level.
Knot: Ghiordes.
Warp: cotton, coarsely spun.
Weft: cotton, coarsely spun, 2 shoots after each row
of knots.
Pile: heavy wool.
Fringe: narrow, woven edge with ordinary or
knotted fringe.
Design: as for Heriz, medallion and corner design
or all-over pattern.
Colours: madder red, blue or beige.
Sizes: mostly large.
Density: 58-155 knots per sq. in. approx. (9-24
knots per sq. cm.).

Meriban   6 ft. 1 in. ×9 ft. 6 in. approx.
(185×290 cm.).
Main design: medallion pattern surrounded by stylized floral design. Main border: Herati patterns. Made after 1945.

MERIBAN

Made in: the village of Meriban south of Heriz (Azerbaijan). 4,590 ft. (1,400 m.) above sea level.
Knot: Ghiordes.
Warp: cotton, coarsely spun.
Weft: cotton, coarsely spun, 2 shoots after each row of knots.
Pile: heavy wool.
Fringe: narrow, woven edge with ordinary or knotted fringe.
Design: as for Heriz and Georavan but predominantly all-over patterns.
Colours: madder red, blue or beige.
Sizes: mostly large.
Density: 58-155 knots per sq. in. approx. (9-24 knots per sq. cm.).

KARAJA

Made in: the area between Tabriz and Ahar in the north-west Heriz district (Azerbaijan). 4,760 ft. (1,450 m.) above sea level.
Knot: Ghiordes.
Warp: cotton.
Weft: cotton; only one shoot after each row of knots, giving the reverse of the carpet a characteristic dotted appearance.
Pile: wool, somewhat stiff.
Fringe: narrow, woven edge with ordinary fringe.
Design: usually three rectilinear medallions, of which two are green or cream-coloured and the central one blue.
Colours: madder red, beige or blue.
Sizes: rugs up to Kellei size, 5 ft. 3 in. × 10 ft. 10 in. approx. (160×330 cm.), or gallery carpets.
Density: 58-194 knots per sq. in. approx. (9-30 knots per sq. cm.).

Karaja   3 ft. 8 in. ×4 ft. 9 in. approx.
(113×145 cm.).
Main design: three geometrical medallions surrounded by stylized floral design. Main border: stars of Caucasian type. Made in the 1930s.

83

Sarab   2 ft. 11 in. ×7 ft. 9 in. approx.
(88 ×235 cm.).
Main design: diamond-shaped rod medallion surrounded by diagonal lattice pattern in a darker shade than the background colour. Dated in the upper part 1351 = 1933. Main border with crab and square pattern. Made in 1933.

SARAB

Made in: the city of Sarab between Tabriz and Ardabil. 4,265 ft. (1,300 m.) above sea level.
Knot: Ghiordes.
Warp: formerly wool, now cotton.
Weft: formerly wool, now cotton, 2 shoots after each row of knots.
Pile: heavy wool.
Fringe: usually artistically plaited edges with short fringe.
Design: diamond-shaped medallions surrounded by rectilinear small patterns. The field is often covered by a diagonal network.
Colours: camel-hair brown predominates but blue or red are also found.
Sizes: rugs or gallery carpets, though ordinary large carpets have begun to appear in recent years.
Density: 58-130 knots per sq. in. approx. (9-20 knots per sq. cm.).

In spite of what is often primitive work, this type is extremely durable besides being interesting for its decorative rectilinear pattern, which also includes stylized animals and figures.

84

BAKSHAISH

Made in: a district to the south-east of Heriz (Azerbaijan).
Knot: Ghiordes.
Warp: cotton.
Weft: cotton, 2 shoots after each row of knots.
Pile: heavy wool.
Fringe: narrow, woven edge with ordinary fringe.
Design: Herati pattern with or without medallion. The newer carpets often have more geometrical patterns like those from the Heriz area.
Colours: dark blue or madder red.
Sizes: mostly oblong up to 8 ft. 2 in. × 14 ft. 9 in. approx. (250 × 450 cm.).
Density: 58-194 knots per sq. in. approx. (9-30 knots per sq. cm.).

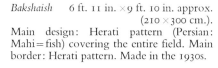

Bakshaish   6 ft. 11 in. × 9 ft. 10 in. approx.
(210 × 300 cm.).
Main design: Herati pattern (Persian: Mahi = fish) covering the entire field. Main border: Herati pattern. Made in the 1930s.

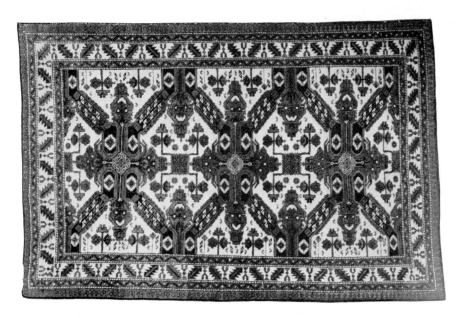

ARDABIL

Made in: the city of Ardabil near the Caspian Sea. 3,610 ft. (1,100 m.) above sea level.

Knot: Ghiordes.

Warp: wool or cotton.

Weft: wool or cotton, 2 shoots after each row of knots.

Pile: fine, somewhat stiff wool.

Fringe: narrow, woven edge with ordinary fringe.

Design: recent pieces use Caucasian patterns such as the Kazak and Shirvan designs with all their geometric elements. The older pieces have rectilinear diamond designs and medallion patterns resembling Tabriz.

Colours: red or beige.

Sizes: rugs, gallery and Kellei 5 ft. 10 in. × 9 ft. 10 in. approx. (180 × 300 cm.).

Density: 139-236 knots per sq. in. approx. (20-35 knots per sq. cm.).

The Ardabil carpet in the Victoria and Albert Museum has nothing to do with carpet-making in this district. The name is used because the carpet used to lie in the mosque in Ardabil. The name Ardabil has also come to be used for gallery carpets in general since both the neighbouring Sarab and Ardabil manufacture a large number of these.

JOSHAGHAN

Made in: the city of Joshaghan, 74 miles (120 km.) north of Isfahan, quite near Kashan.

Knot: Sehna.

Warp: cotton.

Weft: cotton, 2 shoots after each row of knots.

Pile: heavy, fine quality wool.

Fringe: narrow, woven edge and ordinary fringe at either end.

Design: geometric diamond design containing the Mina-Khani design, Guli Henna and weeping willow pattern. Together with these there are also found medallion and corner designs, also geometrically executed.

Colours: madder red, blue or beige.

Sizes: rugs and up to 11 ft. 6 in. × 19 ft. 8 in. approx. (350 × 600 cm.).

Density: 77-433 knots per sq. in. approx. (12-64 knots per sq. cm.).

The method of production, patterns and colours of these carpets have been carefully preserved. They are counted among the best types of pattern in Persia and wonderful qualities were produced in the time of Shah Abbas.

In recent years the city has been subjected to earthquakes and floods so that production is not large. Moreover, knotting over 4 warp threads has been found in modern pieces.

Joshaghan

4 ft. 4 in. ×
6 ft. 11 in. approx.
(132 × 210 cm.).
Main design: stepped
and contoured
diamond medallion
enclosing a lattice
work of Mina-Khani
flowers; stepped and
contoured corners.
The field has a design
with bunches of
diamonds with Guli
Henna and Mina-
Khani flowers. Main
border with double
zig-zag pattern
enclosing floral
design; inner and
outer guards reciprocal
pattern. Made in the
1930s.

87

Saruk   4 ft. 5 in. ×6 ft. 8 in. approx.
(135 ×204 cm.).
Main design: rod medallion and
corners contrasting with the background colour; the entire field has
an all-over pattern with lotus flowers.
Main border: Herati. Made in the
1920s.

Kashan
4 ft. 5 in. ×6 ft. 11 in. approx.
(136 ×210 cm.).
Main design: medallion with rounded edges enclosing a palace design.
The field has an all-over pattern with
lotus and Mina-Khani design. Four
vases protrude from the borders with
flower and bird design. The main
border has a floral pattern and cartouches with palace design. Made
after 1945.

SARUK

Made in: Saruk, a community about 30 miles (50
km.) north-west of Araq in west central Persia.
5,580 ft. (1,700 m.) above sea level.
Knot: Sehna.
Warp: cotton.
Weft: cotton, usually dyed blue or red, 2 shoots
after each row of knots.
Pile: soft, fluffy wool.
Fringe: older carpets have a fringe at one end only;
new pieces have a small woven edge and fringe at
either end.
Design: mostly medallions surrounded by tendril
design. Recent carpets have an empty field around
the medallion or a floral design resembling the
Kerman carpets.
Colours: red, pink, beige or dark blue.
Sizes: rugs, gallery and up to 9 ft. 10 in. × 13 ft. 4 in.
approx. (300×400 cm.).
Density: 103-406 knots per sq. in. approx. (16-63
knots per sq. cm.).

Saruk, together with the carpets from Arak,
which are also known as Saruk, is one of the best
known names for export to America and Europe.
A double warp is used and gives the carpets their
typical massiveness and durability.

KASHAN

Made in: the city of Kashan on the road between
Teheran and Isfahan. 3,100 ft. (945 m.) above sea
level.
Knot: Sehna.
Warp: cotton or silk.
Weft: cotton or silk, 2 shoots after each row of
knots.
Pile: a soft wool or silk.
Fringe: narrow, woven edge and thin, tightly
wound fringe at either end.
Design: finely wrought medallion, tree, niche,
hunting and other figures, as well as all-over floral
designs of various types.
Colours: red, blue or beige.
Sizes: rugs and up to 13 ft. 4 in. × 20 ft. approx.
(400×600 cm.).
Density: 139-452 knots per sq. in. approx. (20-70
knots or more per sq. cm.).

This type of carpet is counted among the finest
in Persia. It is made with a double warp. However,
there are some places in the vicinity of Kashan
where rather simple qualities are produced with
knots round four warp threads. These cannot, of
course, be compared with the other pieces from
Kashan but the prices are set accordingly. Chrome
dyes are now the most common.

Arak 7 ft. ×9 ft. 10 in. approx.
(215 × 300 cm.).
Main design: medallion pattern in the
Kerman style. Border: "broken flower"
border, also Kerman type. Made after 1945.

Bahktiari 5 ft. 1 in. ×7 ft. 3 in. approx.
(155 × 222 cm.).
Main design: medallion with rounded
edges, corner sections. The field has an all-
over pattern with lotus and Mina-Khani
flowers. Main border: magnificent lotus
border in the Herati style. This carpet was
made in the vicinity of Isfahan in the 1930s.

BAHKTIARI

Made in: the area between Arak and Isfahan as well
as southwards towards the Zagros mountains by
nomads and settled tribes.
Knot: Ghiordes, sometimes Sehna.
Warp: cotton.
Weft: cotton, one or two shoots after each row
of knots.
Pile: heavy, somewhat stiff wool.
Fringe: narrow, woven edge and ordinary fringe
at either end.
Design: stylized tree and floral designs in oval or
square frames, known as the garden pattern. Nowadays medallions resembling Isfahan are also found.
Colours: red, blue or beige.
Sizes: from Zaronims 3 ft. 4 in. ×4 ft. 2 in. approx.
(100×150 cm.), up to 13 ft. 4 in. × 16 ft. 8 in.
approx. (400×500 cm.).
Density: 58-232 knots per sq. in. approx. (9-36
knots or more per sq. cm.).

Bahktiari made with one shoot between each
row of knots have the same dotted appearance on
their reverse side as Hamadan, Sehna and Karaja.
The weft threads are sometimes dyed blue. This is
one of the more robust types and can be recom-
mended for halls and dining-rooms.

ARAK

Made in: the city of Arak (formerly Sultanabad).
5,770 ft. (1,759 m.) above sea level.
Knot: Sehna.
Warp: cotton.
Weft: cotton, generally dyed blue or red, 2 shoots
after each row of knots.
Pile: fine quality wool.
Fringe: narrow, woven edge with ordinary or
knotted fringe at one end.
Design: chiefly medallion design with empty field
around it, with or without corners; also all-over
floral design with broken floral border, resembling
Kerman.
Colours: pink, red, beige or dark blue.
Sizes: mostly large carpets up to 13 ft. 4 in. ×20 ft.
approx. (400×600 cm.).
Density: 103-309 knots per sq. in. approx. (16-48
knots per sq. cm.).

Production in this city and the neighbourhood
is identical with that in Saruk but the quality and
patterns are intended for the American market,
which requires definite colours and thicknesses.
Europe, too, has become interested in this type and
has imported many carpets of this quality. The
double warp and the strong technique make this a
very durable quality.

Feraghan   6 ft. 3 in. × 14 ft. 4 in. approx.
(190 × 435 cm.).
Main design: Herati pattern. The Herati
pattern is made in two somewhat different
ways, either with a diamond design as in this
carpet or without this design. Main border:
Herati pattern. Made about the turn of the
century.

FERAGHAN

Made in: the district near Arak.
Knot: Sehna.
Warp: cotton.
Weft: cotton, 2 shoots after each row of knots.
Pile: fine wool.
Fringe: narrow, woven edge, fringe at one end only.
Design: Herati pattern with and without medallion
or corners, also rod medallion.
Colours: red, dark blue or beige; border in bottle
green.
Sizes: rugs and up to 8 ft. 4 in. × 16 ft. 8 in. approx.
(250 × 500 cm.).
Density: 77-308 knots per sq. in. approx. (12-48
knots or more per sq. cm.).

Feraghan carpets are now seldom produced and
the above refers to the older pieces. Present-day
carpets from this district are known as Mahal or
Sultanabad (Araq).

HAMADAN

Made in: the city of Hamadan (formerly Ekbatana) and the surrounding district.

Knot: Ghiordes, sometimes over 4 warp threads.

Warp: cotton.

Weft: cotton, often dyed blue, one pass after each row of knots.

Pile: heavy wool.

Fringe: short Kelim edge, as a rule a fringe at one end only.

Design: geometric rod medallions, stylized floral design, Herati and diamond designs. In older pieces the field is often covered by a lattice work in tone with the basic colour.

Colours: madder red, beige, dark blue and camel-hair brown.

Sizes: rugs, gallery and up to 10 ft. × 20 ft. approx. (300 × 600 cm.).

Density: 58-161 knots per sq. in. approx. (9-25 knots per sq. cm.).

The district has more than 30,000 looms and annual production is considerable. Many places have given their names to the various carpets. Some of the best known are Asadabad, Bibikabad, Borchalou, Dergezin, Huseinabad, Injilas, Karagheus, Kemere, Khamseh, Komat, Maslaghan, Sagheh, Sarderud, Saveh, Shahsavan, Tafresh and Tuiserkan (see pages 202-204).

Hamadan   4 ft. 5 in. × 6 ft. 11 in. approx.
(135 × 211 cm.).
Main design: stepped rod medallion, the corners form a niche at either end, i.e., a double Mihrab = double prayer niches. Main border with stylized floral design. Innermost border has a border pattern that is typical of the carpets from Kurdistan. Made after 1945.

Semnan   4 ft. 5 in. ×6 ft. 7 in. approx.
(134×201 cm.).
Main design: 8-pointed medallion surrounded by two panel designs and four semi-circular medallions. The field has an all-over pattern with lotus flowers. Main border with arabesque and lotus pattern. Made in the 1920s.

Teheran   4 ft. 3 in. ×6 ft. 8 in. approx.
(129×202 cm.).
Main design: niche pattern with vase, tree and bird designs. Two hares at the bottom of the field. Main border: lotus pattern. Made in the 1920s.

TEHERAN

Made in: the central district, around Teheran, the capital of Persia.
Knot: Sehna, also Ghiordes.
Warp: cotton.
Weft: cotton, 2 shoots after each row of knots.
Pile: fine quality wool.
Fringe: narrow, woven edge and ordinary fringe at either end.
Design: generally medallion and floral design resembling Tabriz, panel and niche design and also patterns with animals and figures.
Colours: red, pink, blue or beige.
Sizes: rugs and up to 10 ft.×18 ft. 4 in. approx. (300×550 cm.).
Density: 213-498 knots per sq. in. approx. (33-77 knots or more per sq. cm.).

No carpets are now made in Teheran itself. Production has shifted almost entirely to the nearby town of Qum and its surroundings. The Teheran carpets are often mistaken for better quality Tabriz, which they closely resemble. However, the wool in Teheran pieces is somewhat softer when the pile is the same length and trimmed short. It is easier to distinguish between the older carpets in that Tabriz pieces have the side edges woven flat while the Teheran carpet has oversewn edges.

SEMNAN

Made in: the city of Semnan, approx. 124 miles (200 km.) east of Teheran. 4,370 ft. (1,333 m.) above sea level.
Knot: Sehna.
Warp: cotton.
Weft: cotton, 2 shoots after each row of knots.
Pile: heavy wool.
Fringe: short Kelim and ordinary fringe at either end.
Design: medallion or flower design, resembling that of Teheran but not so delicate.
Colours: light red, blue or beige.
Sizes: rugs and up to 8 ft. 10 in.×11 ft. 10 in. approx. (270×360 cm.).
Density: 77-308 knots per sq. in. approx. (12-48 knots per sq. cm.).

96

Qum 4 ft. 7 in. ×6 ft. 6 in. approx. (140 × 199 cm.). Main design: the "garden pattern", in which the dividing lines symbolize the irrigation channels with trees and flowers growing in the squares between. Main border: Mina-Khani design. Made after 1945.

QUM

Made in: the town of Qum, approx. 93 miles (150 km.) south of Teheran. 3,444 ft. (1,050 m.) above sea level.

Knot: Sehna.

Warp: cotton or silk.

Weft: cotton or silk; 2 shoots after each row of knots.

Pile: fine but somewhat rough wool or silk.

Fringe: narrow, woven edge and ordinary fringe at either end.

Design: mostly all-over floral design, large Mir-Ibotha pattern, medallion, cypresses as well as vase and bird design, nowadays also the garden pattern.

Colours: beige, red or blue ground colour.

Sizes: rugs and up to 8 ft. 4 in. × 13 ft. 4 in. approx. (250 × 400 cm.).

Density: 193-309 knots per sq. in. approx. (30-48 knots per sq. cm.).

Qum is one of the holy cities of Persia and known for its mosques and graves, where great men rest, among them Shah Abbas, the great patron of carpet-making. The tradition of carpet-making is not very old here, having begun during the 1920s. The quality and execution are highly reminiscent of Kashan.

LURISTAN

Made by: a nomad tribe from the Lur district, south-west of Isfahan on the border with Iraq.

Knot: Ghiordes or Sehna.

Warp: wool and goats' hair.

Weft: wool and goats' hair, 2 shoots after each row of knots.

Pile: heavy, somewhat stiff wool.

Fringe: dyed, woven edge and usually a braided fringe at either end.

Design: rectilinear pattern as well as diamond-shaped hook and stepped medallions, resembling the patterns in Kashgai carpets.

Luristan 5 ft. 8 in. × 10 ft. 8 in. approx. (173 × 326 cm.). Main design: three diamond-shaped rod medallions with hook pattern surrounded by pattern resembling Mir-Ibotha. Main border with stylized floral design, inner and outermost guards of the Kurdish type. Made about 1910.

Colours: dark blue or red.

Sizes: rugs and oblong pieces up to 6 ft. 8 in. × 8 ft. 4 in. approx. (200 × 500 cm.).

Density: 77-154 knots per sq. in. approx. (12-24 knots per sq. cm.).

Lilihan 3 ft. 6 in. ×4 ft. 9 in. approx.
(105×146 cm.).
Main design: scalloped medallion with corner sections in a similar style. Stylized lotus flowers protrude from each end of the medallion as well as along the sides from each corner. Main border with flower and stem pattern. Made after 1945.

LILIHAN

Made in: Lilihan, a community 38–50 miles (60–80 km.) south of Arak in the Kemere district.
Knot: Sehna, though Ghiordes is also used.
Warp: cotton.
Weft: cotton, one or two shoots after each row of knots.
Pile: wool.
Fringe: narrow, woven edge and ordinary fringe at either end.
Design: generally large palm-like leaf design or medallion design.
Colours: pink, blue, beige or red.
Sizes: mostly rugs, a few larger pieces up to 10 ft.× 13 ft. 4 in. approx. (300×400 cm.).
Density: 77–231 knots per sq. in. approx. (12–36 knots per sq. cm.).

Malayer 4 ft. 4 in. ×6 ft. 9 in. approx.
(132×205 cm.).
Main design: rod medallion and corner design, here in the form of a quarter medallion. The all-over pattern on the field is dominated by Mina-Khani flowers and a stylized tendril design, typical of rugs from this and the Saruk district. Made after 1945.

MALAYER

Made in: the town of Malayer, approximately 62 miles (100 km.) south of Hamadan. 6,560 ft. (1,998 m.) above sea level.
Knot: Ghiordes, though Sehna is also found.
Warp: cotton.
Weft: cotton, 1 or 2 shoots between each row of knots.
Pile: wool.

Kazvin 4 ft. 5 in. ×6 ft. 9 in. approx.
(133 ×205 cm.).
Main design: curvilinear medallion-and-corner design. The field has an all-over pattern with lotus and Mina-Khani flowers, with the Mir-Ibotha pattern in the corners. Main border with lotus and pairs of Mir-Ibotha patterns. Made in the 1930s.

Fringe: narrow, woven edge, fringe at one end only.
Design: stylized floral design or rectilinear medallions resembling the Saruk carpets.
Colours: blue, pink, red or beige.
Sizes: mostly rugs.
Density: 103-316 knots per sq. in. (16-49 knots per sq. cm.).

Another less well-known name in this district is Jozan, with a quality comparable with Saruk and Malayer. The pattern is of a softer type than Malayer, with gracious vase designs or medallions with or without corner (see page 203).

KAZVIN

Made in: the town of Kazvin approximately 93 miles (150 km.) north-west of Teheran. 4,380 ft. (1,335 m.) above sea level.
Knot: Ghiordes.
Warp: cotton.
Weft: cotton, 2 shoots after each row of knots.
Pile: wool, sometimes mechanically spun.
Fringe: narrow, woven edge and ordinary fringe at either end.
Design: flowing tree, vase and medallion designs, much the same type as Kashan but more crudely executed.
Colours: blue, pink or beige.
Sizes: mostly rugs but a few large pieces up to approximately 8 ft. 10 in.×12 ft. 9 in. (270×360 cm.).
Density: 103-309 knots per sq. in. approx. (16-48 knots per sq. cm.).

Nain. See next page.

NAIN

Made in: the town of Nain approx. 62 miles (100 km.) east of Isfahan.

Knot: Sehna.

Warp: cotton or silk.

Weft: cotton or silk, 2 shoots after each row of knots.

Pile: finest quality wool.

Fringe: short Kelim and ordinary fringe at either end.

Design: similar to Isfahan but mostly tree and bird design, with or without niche, as well as medallion and lotus flower design.

Colours: yellowish-red, light blue or beige.

Sizes: all up to 11 ft. 8 in. × 18 ft. 4 in. approx. (350 × 550 cm.).

Density: 290-645 knots per sq. in. approx. (45-100 knots or more per sq. cm.).

The carpets from this district are known for being the most tightly knotted in the whole of Persia.

SERABAND

Made in: a district south-west of Arak, comprising about 300 small communities.

Knot: Ghiordes or Sehna.

Warp: cotton.

Weft: cotton, often dyed blue, 2 shoots after each row of knots.

Pile: heavy wool.

Fringe: narrow, woven edge, fringe at one end only.

Design: only one pattern, known as the Mir-Ibotha design with or without medallions and corners. The pattern is arranged crosswise with the tip pointing to the left in one row and to the right in the next.

Colours: madder red or blue, occasionally beige.

Sizes: all up to 11 ft. 8 in. × 16 ft. 8 in. approx. (350 × 500 cm.).

Density: 58-161 knots per sq. in. approx. (9-25 knots per sq. cm.).

The finest Seraband carpets are often known as Mir. Production of the famous Mir carpets came to an end late in the 19th century when the district was destroyed in an earthquake. These carpets are regarded as valuable and are in any case extremely rare.

The present day Seraband carpet cannot be compared with the old Mir carpet in quality. The pattern is the same, the Mir-Ibotha design.

Nain 5 ft. 1 in. × 7 ft. 6 in. approx. (155 × 230 cm.).
Main design: sixteen-pointed medallion and a tendril design with lotus flowers, characteristic of rugs from Nain and Isfahan. Main border with arabesque and lotus pattern. There are approx. 1,230,000 knots per sq. m. Made after 1945. (Reproduced in colour on preceding page.)

Seraband 6 ft. 11 in. × 10 ft. 7 in. approx. (210 × 322 cm.).
Main design: Mir-Ibotha pattern. Main border: Schekeri or Mir border. Outer and inner guards have a reciprocal pattern, i.e., the same design done in two colours. Made after 1945.

Mahal 8 ft. 5 in. ×11 ft. approx. (260×335 cm.).
Main design: diamond-shaped medallion with surrounding Herati pattern, corners with stylized arabesque design on light ground. Main border: wavy leaf and flower border. Made after 1945.

Isfahan 4 ft. 6 in. ×7 ft. 2 in. approx. (138×220 cm.).
Main design: vase with tree, flower and bird pattern. Main border with floral pattern, birds and other animal designs. Made in the 1930s.

ISFAHAN

Made in: Isfahan, the former capital of Persia, approximately 248 miles (400 km.) south of Teheran on the road to Shiraz. 4,690 ft. (1,430 m.) above sea level.
Knot: Sehna.
Warp: cotton or silk.
Weft: cotton or silk, 2 shoots after each row of knots.
Pile: wool, short and stiff but of fine quality; sometimes partly or wholly of silk.
Fringe: narrow, woven edge and fringe at either end.
Design: pointed medallions with corners, niche, tree and bird design. Beautifully executed small lotus flower pattern surrounded by tendrils.
Colours: deep red, dark and light blue or beige.
Sizes: all up to 15 ft. ×18 ft. 4 in. approx. (450×550 cm.).
Density: 129-516 knots per sq. in. approx. (20-80 knots per sq. cm.).

Isfahan is the classical carpet town, chiefly because Shah Abbas, the great patron of carpet-making, made it his capital. Present-day production is still admirable in quality, and carpets are made with about 900 knots per sq. in. (140 per sq. cm.). The colours are possibly somewhat hard, but the patterns are as artistic as ever.

MAHAL

Made in: the districts of Mahallat, Muskabad and Dulakhor, all in the Arak weaving area.
Knot: Sehna, also Ghiordes, often over 4 warp threads.
Warp: cotton, coarsely spun.
Weft: cotton, usually dyed blue, 2 shoots after each row of knots.
Pile: heavy wool, good quality.
Fringe: narrow, woven edge with fringe at one end.
Design: Guli Henna, Mina-Khani, Herati or medallion design with or without corners.
Colours: terracotta red, beige or dark blue.
Sizes: mostly large, up to 16 ft. 8 in. × 23 ft. 4 in. approx. (500×700 cm.).
Density: 58-194 knots per sq. in. approx. (9-30 knots per sq. cm.).

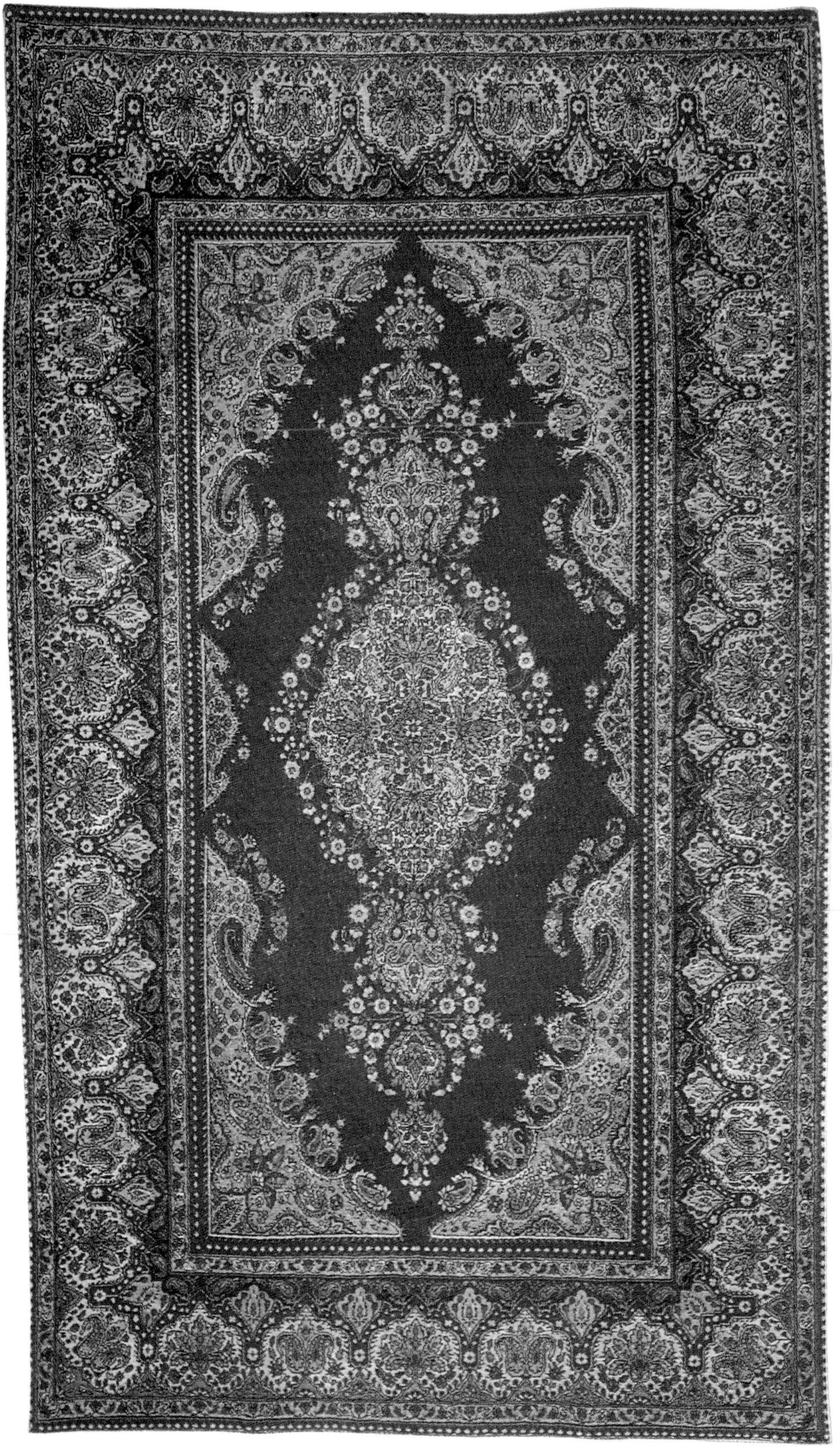

Kerman   4 ft. 2 in. ×7 ft. approx.
(127 ×213 cm.).
Main design: oblong rod medallion and scalloped corners. Main border with lotus and Mir-Ibotha design. Made in the 1930s.

KERMAN

Made in: Kerman, provincial capital. 6,100 ft. (1,860 m.) above sea level.
Knot: Sehna.
Warp: cotton.
Weft: cotton, 3 shoots after each row of knots.
Pile: soft, fine quality wool.
Fringe: narrow, woven edge and usually a fringe at either end.
Design: older pieces have tree, animal and human figure designs, medallion and rose patterns. The newer carpets have medallions and bouquet designs with empty monochrome field around the medallion or all-over floral design.
Colours: red, pink, blue or beige.
Sizes: all, including vast pieces.
Density: 129-406 knots per sq. in. approx. (20-63 knots per sq. cm.).

Kerman produces the most refined and elegant carpets in the whole of Persia. The weavers have an inherited sense of colour and always match the colours of the patterns to the basic colour. This is seldom the case elsewhere in Persia, where the same pattern colours are used irrespective of whether the ground is blue, red or beige. Moreover, vegetable dyes are almost always used. America has been the largest buyer for more than forty years and has managed to influence production so that thickness, pattern and colour have been adapted to American taste. Previously, Kerman carpets had a different colour scale, were thinner and used yarns of quite different thicknesses. The wool is of excellent quality and the roller beam type of loom used in this district makes it possible to produce large, even carpets.

Abadeh   3 ft. 9 in. ×5 ft. 1 in. approx.
(115 ×155 cm.).
Main design: diamond pattern, enclosing large floral design which is also included in the four corners. The entire field has an all-over pattern with tree and flower designs. Main border: distinct lotus border. Made after 1945.

ABADEH

Made in: the town of Abadeh (Fars), north of Shiraz on the road to Isfahan. 6,600 ft. (2,011 m.) above sea level.
Knot: Sehna.
Warp: cotton.
Weft: cotton, 2 shoots after each row of knots.
Pile: stiff, heavy wool.
Fringe: short, Kelim and ordinary or knotted fringe at either end.
Design: similar to Kashgai with diamond-shaped medallions and stylized flower and vase design.
Colours: brick red, blue or beige.
Sizes: rugs and up to 5 ft. 9 in. ×11 ft. 8 in. approx. (180 ×350 cm.).
Density: 58-271 knots per sq. in. approx. (9-42 knots per sq. cm.).

SHIRAZ

Made in: the city of Shiraz in southern Persia.
4,920 ft. (1,500 m.) above sea level.
Knot: Sehna, though Ghiordes is also found.
Warp: wool and goats' hair.
Weft: wool and goats' hair, 2 shoots after each row
of knots.
Pile: a lustrous type of wool.
Fringe: narrow, woven edge and ordinary fringe at
either end.
Design: rectilinear pattern and medallions as well as
diamond design; in older pieces Mir-Ibotha and
vertical stripe design.
Colours: madder red or blue.
Sizes: rugs and up to 8 ft. 4 in. × 11 ft. 8 in. approx.
(250 × 350 cm.).
Density: 39-156 knots per sq. in. approx. (6-24 knots
per sq. cm.).

The Fars district has a population of about one
million, of whom one third are nomads. These
spend about eight months of the year in the mountain
districts and in the late autumn they descend to the
coastal districts south of Shiraz. All the nomad tribes
make saddle bags in various sizes. The front of one
of these bags is like a small rug and the back panel is
woven plain. In the tent the saddle bag is used to hold
small articles.

YEZD

Made in: the town of Yezd, north-west of Kerman
on the road to Nain. 4,070 ft. (1,240 m.) above sea
level.
Knot: Ghiordes, though Sehna is also found.
Warp: cotton.
Weft: cotton, dyed blue, 2 shoots after each row of
knots.
Pile: fine quality wool.
Fringe: narrow, woven edge and fringe at either end.
Design: similar to the older Kerman, medallion and
corners, oval panels with floral design and Herati
pattern.
Colours: blue, red or beige.
Sizes: mostly large carpets up to 11 ft. 8 in. × 16 ft.
8 in. approx. (350 × 500 cm.).
Density: 129-309 knots per sq. in. approx. (20-48
knots per sq. cm.).

Kashgai 5 ft. 9 in. ×9 ft. 8 in. approx.
(175 ×295 cm.).
Main design: five diamonds that form an unusual zig-zag pattern with the half-diamonds down the sides. The light field has an all-over design with flowers, birds and other animals. Main border: wavy with floral design, the outer guard has a diamond pattern. Made around the turn of the century.

Afshar 4 ft. 10 in. ×6 ft. 5 in. approx.
(148 ×195 cm.).
Main design: two diamonds with hook pattern in a geometrical field, corners with Mir-Ibotha pattern. Main border with stylized floral design. Made after 1945.

KASHGAI

Made by: nomadic tribe, numbering approximately 250,000, which wanders among the mountains north of Shiraz in the summer, and to the west and south of Shiraz in the winter (Fars).
Knot: Ghiordes, though Sehna is also found.
Warp: wool and goats' hair.
Weft: wool and goats' hair, 2 shoots after each row of knots.
Pile: heavy wool.
Fringe: wide, woven edge and ordinary or knotted fringe at either end.
Design: rectilinear design, diamond-shaped medallions and corners, stylized animals and human figures.
Colours: terracotta red or blue.
Sizes: rugs or Kellei up to 6 ft. 3 in. ×11 ft. 8 in. approx. (190 ×350 cm.).
Density: 58-236 knots per sq. in. approx. (9-35 knots per sq. cm.).

These carpets are of much heavier type than the Shiraz carpets.

AFSHAR

Made by: semi-nomads around Saidabad (Kerman).
Knot: Sehna, though Ghiordes is also found.
Warp: cotton.
Weft: cotton, 2 shoots after each row of knots.
Pile: wool.
Fringe: narrow, woven edge and fringe at either end.
Design: diamond-shaped stepped medallions, stylized bird design, Mir-Ibotha patterns.
Colours: red, pink, blue, yellow or beige.
Sizes: rugs and up to 6 ft. 3 in. ×9 ft. 10 in. approx. (190 ×300 cm.).
Density: 77-273 knots per sq. in. approx. (12-42 knots per sq. cm.).

III

112

Qain   3 ft. 7 in. × 5 ft. 5 in. approx.
               (110 × 164 cm.).
Main design: Mir-Ibotha pattern. Main
border: narrow flower tendril border. Made
at the turn of the century.

QAIN

Made in: the town of Qain, south of Meshed in the district of Khurasan. 4,920 ft. (1,500 m.) above sea level.
Knot: Sehna.
Warp: cotton, coarsely spun.
Weft: cotton, 2 shoots after each row of knots.
Pile: wool.
Fringe: narrow, woven edge and fringe at either end.
Design: Mir-Ibotha and floral design, also medallion pattern.
Colours: cochineal red, blue or beige.
Sizes: rugs and up to 10 ft. × 13 ft. 4 in. approx. (300 × 400 cm.), also Kellei.
Density: 97-348 knots per sq. in. approx. (15-54 knots per sq. cm.).

Birjand   4 ft. × 6 ft. 2 in. approx.
                  (122 × 188 cm.).
Main design: vase and floral design, dominated by five large carnations. Main border: leaf and flower design surrounded by secondary reciprocal zig-zag border.

BIRJAND

Made in: the town of Birjand, south of Qain in the district of Khurasan. 5,215 ft. (1,590 m.) above sea level.
Knot: Sehna.
Warp: cotton, coarsely spun.
Weft: cotton, 2 shoots after each row of knots.
Pile: heavy wool.
Fringe: narrow, woven edge and fringe at either end.
Design: medallion design and all-over floral design.
Colours: cochineal red or beige.
Sizes: mostly large carpets.
Density: 77-273 knots per sq. in. approx. (12-42 knots per sq. cm.).

114

Durukhsh   3 ft. 4 in. × 4 ft. 7 in. approx.
             (102 × 138 cm.).
Main design: stepped medallion and corners.
Main border: lotus pattern. Made around
1910.

Turkbaff   10 ft. × 14 ft. approx.
             (305 × 425 cm.).
Main design: medallion with flower tendrils
and corners. Main border with lotus and
Mina-Khani pattern. Made after 1935.

TURKBAFF

Made in: the Meshed district of Khurasan, production
in the Turkish manner.
Knot: Ghiordes.
Warp: cotton, coarsely spun.
Weft: cotton, technique similar to the Khurasan
carpets.
Pile: heavy wool.
Fringe: narrow, woven edge and ordinary fringe at
either end.
Design: like Meshed, medallion and flower design.
Colours: cochineal red, blue or beige.
Sizes: large carpets.
Density: 77-236 knots per sq. in. approx. (12-35
knots per sq. cm.).

This type is made exclusively with the knot
round two warp threads, the weavers using a hooked
knife that makes it impossible to use the "Jufti" knot
round four warp threads. The origin of this type is
attributed to some Tabriz merchants who started
production in Meshed and thereby transferred the
Tabriz technique to the new Turkbaff quality. The
first Turkbaff carpets were made towards the end of
the last century.

DURUKHSH

Made in: Durukhsh, approximately 50 miles (80
km.) north-east of Birjand in the province of Khu-
rasan.
Knot: Sehna.
Warp: cotton.
Weft: cotton, technique like the other Khurasan
types.
Pile: wool.
Fringe: narrow, woven edge and ordinary fringe at
either end.
Design: large medallion surrounded by plain field
and corners or large Mir-Ibotha design. Sometimes
figural patterns.
Colours: cochineal red, pink or beige.
Sizes: rugs and up to 10 ft. × 13 ft. 4 in. approx.
(300 × 400 cm.).
Density: 97-348 knots per sq. in. approx. (15-54
knots per sq. cm.).

116

KHURASAN

Made in: the province of Khurasan in north-east Persia. Collective name for carpets from this district.
Knot: Sehna, sometimes round four warp threads.
Warp: cotton.
Weft: cotton, 2 shoots after each row of knots in modern pieces, previously another technique (see below).
Pile: fine quality wool.
Fringe: narrow, woven edge and fringe at either end.
Design: medallion and corner design on plain ground or Herati or Mir-Ibotha pattern. Sometimes all-over flower design.
Colours: dark cochineal red, blue or beige.
Sizes: mostly large carpets up to 13 ft. 2 in. × 20 ft. approx. (400 × 600 cm.).
Density: 97-348 knots per sq. in. approx. (15-54 knots per sq. cm.).

In the old technique, two thin weft threads were passed after each row of knots but after every third or fourth row an additional pair of heavier weft threads was also passed, giving the back of the carpet a ribbed appearance.

In Khurasan madder red is not used for the ground; the typical violet-red colour comes from cochineal red. The wool from this district is known as the best in all Persia.

Khurasan   8 ft. 5 in. × 11 ft. 2 in. approx.
                  (260 × 340 cm.).
Main design: rod medallion with lotus pattern and corners. Main border: Herati pattern; inner and outer guards have a flower tendril design. Made in the 1930s.

MESHED

Made in: Meshed, the provincial capital (Khurasan). 3,200 ft. (975 m.) above sea level.
Knot: Sehna, sometimes round four warp threads.
Warp: cotton.
Weft: cotton, technique as in Khurasan.
Pile: fine, heavy quality wool.
Fringe: narrow, woven edge and fringe at either end.
Design: medallion and Mir-Ibotha pattern, also all-over flower design.
Colours: dark cochineal red, blue or beige.
Sizes: mostly large carpets, up to 16 ft. 8 in. × 23 ft. 4 in. approx. (500 × 700 cm.).
Density: 77-363 knots per sq. in. approx. (12-56 knots or more per sq. cm.).

Meshed   4 ft. 7 in. × 7 ft. 4 in. approx.
                (138 × 225 cm.).
Main design: medallion with sixteen scallops, surrounded by cartouches with tendril design. Main border with Guli Henna design; inner and outer guards with Mir-Ibotha pattern. Made around 1920.

Bijar 4 ft. 8 in. ×7 ft. 1 in. approx. (141×216 cm.). Main design: diamond medallion with a decorative motif at the top and bottom on a monochrome field surrounded by the Herati pattern. Main border: Herati. Made in the 1930s.

BIJAR (also known as Sarak)

Made in: the town of Bijar in the Gerus district (Kurdistan). 3,870 ft. (1,180 m.) above sea level.
Knot: Ghiordes.
Warp: wool, in modern carpets cotton.
Weft: wool or cotton, 3 shoots after each row of knots.
Pile: heavy wool.
Fringe: fringe at one end only, the woven edges nearest the knots oversewn with red wool.
Design: round or stepped medallions, all-over flower design, Herati pattern and sometimes bird and other animal designs.

Zenjan 4 ft. 4 in. ×6 ft. 9 in. approx. (132×205 cm.). Main design: three large geometrical medallions placed laterally, four smaller medallions without rods. The field decorated with stylized floral and bird designs. Main border with "S" design, surrounded by two borders with Herati pattern. Made in the 1920s.

ZENJAN

Made in: the Kurdistan town of Zenjan, approximately 217 miles (350 km.) south-east of Tabriz on the road towards Kazvin and Teheran. 6,230 ft. (1,900 m.) above sea level.
Warp: cotton, coarsely spun.
Weft: cotton, 2 shoots after each row of knots.
Pile: coarsely spun wool.
Fringe: narrow, woven edge with ordinary or knotted fringe.
Design: small flower and leaf design as well as rectilinear medallions reminiscent of Hamadan.
Colours: red or blue, less frequently beige. Unfortunately, inferior chemical dyes are used to a considerable extent.
Sizes: rugs and up to approx. 5 ft.×8 ft. 4 in. (150×250 cm.).
Density: 77-194 knots per sq. in. approx. (12-30 knots per sq. cm.).

Colours: sombre dark red and blue, occasionally beige.
Sizes: rugs and up to approx. 10 ft.×15 ft. (300×450 cm.).
Density: 58-194 knots per sq. in. approx. (9-30 knots per sq. cm.).

The Bijar carpet is regarded as one of the strongest in Persia. It has a double warp and the weft threads are packed together with a needle-like instrument so that the surface is extremely solid. The great weight of these carpets and the relatively slight looms often produce rather crooked edges.

Sehna   3 ft. 5 in. × 4 ft. 11 in. approx.
(106 × 150 cm.).
Main design: stepped rod medallion with
similar corners, all-over Herati pattern.
Main border: roughly stylized floral design.
Made after 1945.

SEHNA

Made in: the city of Sanandaj (formerly Sehna) near
Bijar. 4,000 ft. (1,220 m.) above sea level.
Knot: Ghiordes, though Sehna is also found.
Warp: cotton or silk.
Weft: cotton or silk, only one shoot after each row
of knots.
Pile: fine but extremely rough wool.
Fringe: narrow, woven edge with ordinary or
knotted fringe at one end.
Design: rectilinear rod medallion, Herati or Mir-
Ibotha pattern; very occasionally a French-type
flower pattern, known in Persia as Guli Frank.
Colours: dark blue, red or beige.
Sizes: rugs and up to approx. 10 ft. 6 in. × 16 ft. 8 in.
(320 × 500 cm.).
Density: 129-516 knots per sq. in. approx. (20-80
knots per sq. cm.).

This type is regarded as one of the better in
Persia. With only one weft thread after each row of
knots it is easily recognized by its dotted reverse.
This is the district of the Sehna Kelim, the foremost
type of Kelim.

120

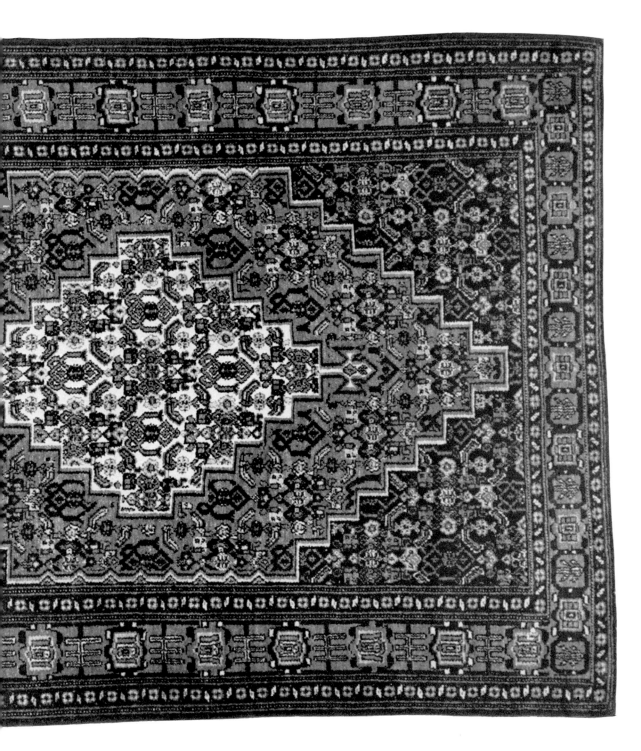

Kurdistan I ft. 8 in. × 2 ft. 6 in. approx.
(50 × 75 cm.).
Main design: roughly drawn medallion.
The pattern runs from side to side as this rug
is wider that it is long. Main border with
floral design, one side border missing (right).
Made in the 1920s.

Kermanshah 7 ft. 11 in. × 12 ft. 8 in.
approx. (240 × 385 cm.).
Main design: rod medallion and corners
resembling Kashan. Vase with floral bouquet
design surrounded by flower tendrils. Main
border: roughly designed Herati border
reminiscent of the Saruk rugs. Made in the
1920s.

KERMANSHAH

Made in: the city of Kermanshah (Kurdistan) on the ancient caravan route to Baghdad. 3,410 ft. (1,140 m.) above sea level.

Knot: Sehna.

Warp: cotton.

Weft: cotton, 2 shoots after each row of knots.

Pile: fine wool.

Fringe: narrow, woven edge and ordinary fringe.

Design: large medallion and groups of flowers as well as artistically designed corners and borders.

Colours: mostly beige or pink with pastel complementary colours.

Sizes: mostly large carpets.

Density: 103-309 knots per sq. in. approx. (16-48 knots per sq. cm.).

Nowadays carpets are not produced in this city and consequently one should be extremely suspicious of carpets that are said to be genuine Kermanshah. A similar quality with this name is made in Tabriz and Arak.

On the other hand, nomads in the mountain districts around Kermanshah produce a quite different type of carpet. This has roughly drawn rectilinear patterns resembling the Caucasian and has wool for both warp and weft. These carpets are seldom exported.

KURDISTAN (nomad)

Made by: nomads in western Persia along the borders of Iraq and Turkey.

Knot: Ghiordes.

Warp: wool and goats' hair.

Weft: wool and goats' hair, 2-4 shoots after each row of knots.

Pile: heavy wool.

Fringe: woven, edge and fringe at one end, the edge usually decorated with a two-coloured over-and-over stitch.

Design: Mina-Khani, Herati and rectilinear diamond and medallion design as well as small ornaments.

Colours: dark, mostly blue or madder red grounds with strongly contrasting colours in the patterns.

Sizes: rugs, gallery and Kellei.

Density: 58-129 knots per sq. in. approx. (9-20 knots per sq. cm.).

The Caucasus

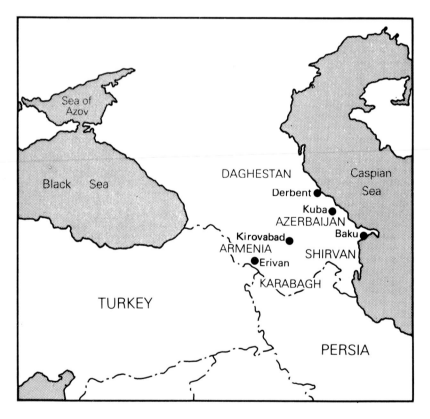

The regions in the Caucasus showing places and districts where carpets are produced.

Azerbaijan:
Kuba
Kirovabad (Gendje, Kazak)
Shirvan
Karabagh
Baku (Khila)

Armenia:
Erivan

Daghestan:
Mikrakh
Akhty
Derbent

From very early times the Caucasus, often a migration route, was overrun and conquered by peoples of many different origins. Two semi-independent states, Georgia and Armenia, both on the Black Sea side of the isthmus, had existed from about the 12th century B.C. The area remained just outside the empires of Alexander the Great and the Romans, but came under Islamic control in the 8th century A.D. The Armenians also pushed in from the south, and Mongolian and Turkish Tartar tribes from the north. In the 13th century the Caucasus was conquered by the Mongols; from the 15th century it was alternately under the rule of the Persians and the Turks. Russia had long been trying to move into the area, and Catherine's II successful peace of 1774 extended the southern borders of Russia beyond the Northern Caucasus to the Kuban and Terek rivers. Having established itself, Russia gradually expanded southwards. The entire Caucasus is now part of the Soviet Union.

The Caucasus Mountains divide North Caucasus from Trans-Caucasus, which comprises the Soviet Republics of Azerbaijan, Armenia and Georgia. There are numerous tribes and a multitude of languages. The industrialized cities are becoming more and more Russian every day.

The Caucasus plays a decisive part in Russia's economy owing to its wealth of minerals: oil, manganese, zinc, barytes, andesite and rare metals.

The region extends from the Black Sea and the Sea of Azov to the Caspian Sea. The best known oil fields and the largest refineries lie around Baku on the Caspian Sea. The oil is shipped from the harbour at Baku or is piped to Batumi on the Black Sea.

The Caucasus range, between the Black and Caspian Seas, is 745 miles (1,200 km.) long and an average of 93 miles (150 km.) wide. The east European winter predominates north of the main ridge but Trans-Caucasus has mild winters and down by the Black Sea the climate is sub-tropical and so is the vegetation—the coastal strip is Russia's Riviera.

In the south the border with Persia follows the river Araxes, which cuts through the Mughan steppe on its way to Kuba. Anyone looking for evidence that culture knows no political boundaries will find it here—no one can tell on which side of the river a Mughan carpet has been made.

Another example is the carpets from the Karabagh

The main design comprises a tree of life
and stylized floral design; the field has a bird
and animal design. The main border is a
highly stylized lotus border. Made at the
turn of the century.

district in Azerbaijan, which have many delicate
patterns reminiscent of the Persian style. The knot is
the Ghiordes and the women do the weaving. Here,
too, people on either side of the boundary are in
close contact with one another.

In the olden days the tiny communities and
villages were isolated from the outside world by the
inaccessibility of the region and consequently the
carpets retained their original patterns and techniques. Modern communications, however, have led
to both patterns and methods of production being
spread to other parts of the country.

Nowadays, carpet-making in the Caucasus is
largely nationalized. Yarn and material for the warp
are supplied ready for use to large, efficient weaving
stations. Production is based on patterns from
classical carpets, the technique is good and the
quality durable. A strong cotton yarn is used for the
warp and consequently the carpets lie well on the
floor. The colours are good and generally come from
vegetable dyes.

A general feature is the rectilinear pattern—which
can be found reproduced in 15th-century paintings.
Highly stylized animals and human figures are sometimes found. The plain woven carpets without a pile
form an interesting group. The best known is the
Sumakh type, which is described here in a special
section together with some variations on the same
technique (see pages 185 and 193).

Carpet-making in the Caucasus, like that in
Persia, has an ancient heritage. The carpets of the
Caucasus are also known for their good quality.

Kuba 4 ft. 9 in. ×7 ft. 1 in. approx.
(145 ×218 cm.).
Main design: dominant pattern resembling
goat horns, known as the Perebedil pattern
after a community to the north of Kuba,
where this pattern is generally used. The
Caucasians call the pattern Burma. It is
supported by a pattern of stylized floral and
star designs. Main border: the crab border
surrounded by flower and carnation
borders. Made after 1945.

KUBA

Made in: the town of Kuba, north of Baku near the
Caspian Sea (Azerbaijan).
Knot: Ghiordes.
Warp: cotton.
Weft: cotton or wool, 2 shoots after each row of
knots.
Pile: heavy wool.
Fringe: narrow, woven edge and an ordinary or a
knotted, plaited fringe at either end.
Design: small geometric design, diamonds or
medallions as well as rectilinear all-over flower
design.
Colours: red, blue or beige.
Sizes: older carpets are usually small, modern ones
up to 6 ft. 8 in. × 10 ft. approx. (200 × 300 cm.).
Density: 77-236 knots per sq. in. approx. (12-35
knots per sq. cm.).

GENDJE

Made in: Kirovabad (formerly Gendje) and the
surrounding district (Azerbaijan).
Knot: Ghiordes.
Warp: wool in older carpets, cotton in newer ones.
Weft: wool in older carpets, cotton in newer ones,
with up to eight shoots after each row of knots.
Pile: coarsely spun wool.
Fringe: ordinary woven edge with knotted fringe at
either end; some older carpets have a fringe at one
end only.
Design: very like the Kazak carpets with three
medallions, the middle one usually being larger
than the other two; also octagon design.

Gendje 3 ft. 1 in. ×5 ft. 9 in. approx.
(96 ×175 cm.).
Main design: stepped medallion with hook
pattern, surrounded by stylized floral design,
two comb designs at one end. Main border:
wine glass and leaf pattern; inner and outer
guards: "S" design. Made in the 1930s.

Colours: blue, madder red or dark blue.
Sizes: Kellei size up to 5 ft. 9 in.×8 ft. 7 in. approx.
(175 × 260 cm.).
Density: 39-123 knots per sq. in. approx. (6-19 knots
per sq. c.m)

Main design: medallion, diamond, tree and floral design. The corners form double Mihrabs. Main border: the Shirvan border. Made after 1945.

Shirvan   3 ft. 5 in. × 5 ft. approx.
(104 × 152 cm.).
Main design: the Perebedil and two vertical rows of stylized camel designs filled out with geometrically drawn floral design. Main border: a double hook border, which is a typical Shirvan border. Made in the 1920s.

SHIRVAN

Made in: the district of Shirvan (Azerbaijan).
Knot: Ghiordes.
Warp: cotton.
Weft: cotton or wool, 2 shoots after each row of knots.
Pile: fine quality wool.
Fringe: narrow, woven edge and an ordinary or a knotted, plaited fringe at either end.
Design: geometric medallion surrounded by small devices or small geometric devices alone; sometimes also an angular niche design.
Colours: dark blue or red.
Sizes: mostly rugs but also up to 6 ft. 8 in. × 10 ft. approx. (200 × 300 cm.). The older carpets are mostly Kelleis, 5 ft. × 10 ft. 6 in. approx. (150 × 320 cm).
Density: 77-300 knots per sq. in. approx. (12-48 knots per sq. cm.).

Shirvan is one of the best known types of carpet from the Caucasus and is famous for its good qualities and wealth of patterns. Common patterns are the eight-pointed star, the spider, swastika square, cross, hooked pattern, "S" design and stylized animals and human figures. The borders are decorated with the wine glass device, the crab and the most common Shirvan border (see page 39).

ERIVAN

Made in: the town and district of Erivan (Armenia).
Knot: Ghiordes.
Warp: cotton.
Weft: cotton, 2 shoots after each row of knots.
Pile: heavy, somewhat stiff wool.
Fringe: narrow, woven edge and ordinary fringe at either end.
Design: similar to Kazak and Gendje, rectilinear octagons and medallions, but also the small stylized flower design of the Shirvan.
Colours: blue or red ground; the red is given an unusual brown shade by this district's water, which is used to rinse the yarn after dyeing.
Sizes: mostly rugs.
Density: 77-129 knots per sq. in. approx. (12-20 knots per sq. cm.).

133

Karabagh 3 ft. 8 in. × 10 ft. 7 in. approx. (112 × 323 cm.). Main design: geometrically stylized floral and octagon design. A double comb design between the octagons. Main border: octagons and double comb design. Made in the 1930s.

KARABAGH

Made in: the district of Karabagh (Azerbaijan).

Knot: Ghiordes.

Warp: cotton or wool.

Weft: cotton or wool, 2 shoots after each row of knots.

Pile: somewhat stiff wool.

Fringe: narrow, woven edge and ordinary fringe at either end.

Design: this type, too, sometimes has the soft patterns of the Persian carpet with medallions, flowers and occasionally human figures; however, highly stylized floral designs are most common in typical Caucasian patterns.

Colours: dark blue, madder red, violet red or beige.

Sizes: mostly oblong, up to 8 ft. 4 in. × 18 ft. 4 in. approx. (250 × 550 cm.).

Density: 58-161 knots per sq. in. approx. (9-25 knots per sq. cm.).

KHILA

Made in: the Baku district (Azerbaijan).

Knot: Ghiordes.

Warp: cotton.

Weft: cotton, 2 shoots after each row of knots.

Pile: fine quality wool.

Fringe: narrow, woven edge and ordinary fringe at either end.

Design: graceful, Mir-Ibotha patterns with or without rectilinear medallion; sometimes half the medallion is depicted as a zig-zag pattern along the innermost guard of the sides. Occasionally an all-over flower design.

Colours: dark blue.

Sizes: Kellei up to 6 ft. 11 in. × 11 ft. 8 in. approx. (210 × 350 cm.).

Density: 77-271 knots per sq. in. approx. (12-42 knots per sq. cm.).

These carpets are very rare. Their design is one of the few exceptions to the normally strict geometric patterns of the Caucasus.

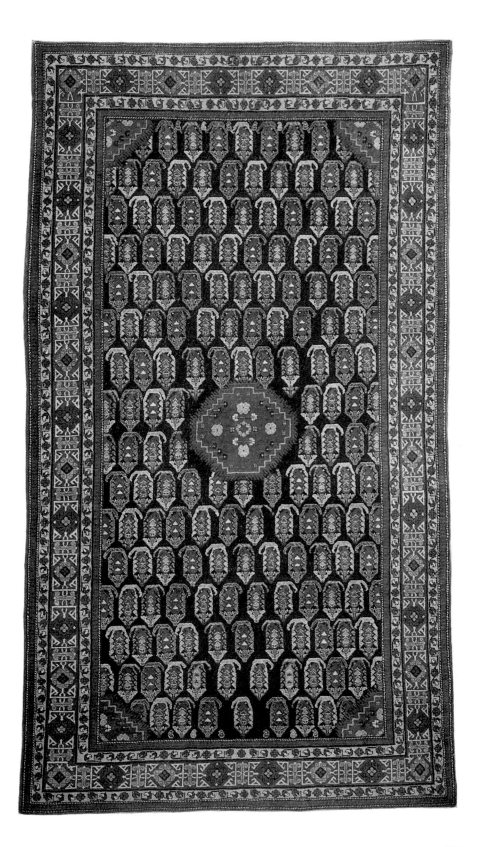

Khila   5 ft. 5 in. ×
9 ft. 9 in. approx.
(165 × 298 cm.).
Main design: Mir–Ibotha
pattern and a small stepped
medallion. Main border:
Shirvan border. Made after
1945.

135

136

Mikrakh   5 ft. 1 in. ×7 ft. 9 in. approx.
(155×235 cm.).
Main design: three toothed medallions and
stylized flower design. Main border: crab
border. Made after 1945.

Kazak   5 ft. 1 in. ×7 ft. 10 in. approx.
(155×238 cm.).
Main design: diamond-shaped rod medallion and six large stylized leaf designs, with a
number of "S" designs in the field. Main
border: series of squares with bird-like
designs. Made around the turn of the
century.

KAZAK

Made in: the district of Kirovabad and up towards
the river Kura with the small towns of Karasachkal
and Taus as the northern limit (Azerbaijan).
Knot: Ghiordes.
Warp: dyed wool in older carpets, cotton in newer
ones.
Weft: dyed wool in older carpets, cotton in newer
ones, with 2-4 or more shoots after each row of
knots.
Pile: fine though heavy wool.
Fringe: generally a knotted, plaited fringe at either
end.
Design: large stepped or rectilinear octagon medallions, surrounded by stylized animals and human
figures together with other typical geometric star,
cross, tree or "S" patterns.
Colours: dark blue or madder red.
Sizes: some rugs, or some square or Kellei sizes up to
6 ft. × 8 ft. 7 in. approx. (180×260 cm.).
Density: 58-154 knots per sq. in. approx. (9-24 knots
per sq. cm.).

The weft technique gives the backs of these
carpets a characteristic ribbed appearance. In this
they resemble the Gendje carpet from the area south
of Kirovabad. The pile is generally longer in this
type of carpet than in other Caucasian pieces; the
only exception is Gendje, which has the same character as Kazak.

MIKRAKH

Made in: the village of Mikrakh (Daghestan).
Knot: Ghiordes.
Warp: cotton.
Weft: cotton, 2 shoots after each row of knots.
Pile: heavy wool.
Fringe: narrow, woven edge and knotted fringe at
either end.
Design: three toothed diamond medallions on an
almost plain ground or two zig-zag geometrical
designs down the length of the carpet, forming a
number of diamond-shaped medallions; common
small Caucasian designs are used to fill in.
Colours: blue, golden yellow, red, green, beige or
brown.
Sizes: rugs and up to 5 ft. 10 in. × 8 ft. 4 in. approx.
(175×250 cm.).
Density: 77-194 knots per sq. in. approx. (12-30
knots per sq. cm.).

AKHTY

Made in: the district of Akhty (Daghestan).
Knot: Ghiordes.
Warp: cotton.
Weft: cotton, 2 shoots after each row of knots.
Pile: fine quality wool.
Fringe: ordinary woven edge with knotted fringe at either end.
Design: the field has three rectilinear medallions, decorated with a hooked ray design.
Colours: madder red, dark blue or beige.
Sizes: rugs and up to 5 ft. 10 in. × 8 ft. 4 in. approx. (175 × 250 cm.).
Density: 103-194 knots per sq. in. approx. (16-30 knots per sq. cm.).

Akhty   4 ft. 6 in. ×7 ft. approx. (137 × 212 cm.).
Main design: three medallions with sunray pattern and some stylized animal designs in the field. Main border: crab pattern. Made after 1945.

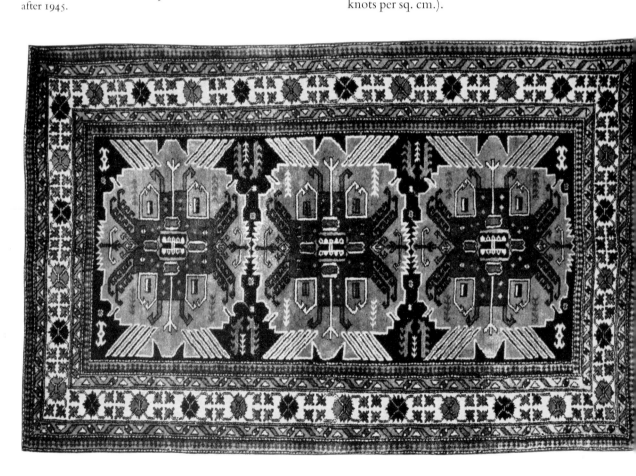

DERBENT

Made in: the district around Derbent, the provincial capital of Daghestan.

Knot: Ghiordes.

Warp: wool in older carpets, cotton in newer ones.

Weft: wool in older carpets, cotton in newer ones, 2 shoots after each row of knots.

Pile: heavy wool.

Fringe: narrow, woven edge and knotted fringe at either end.

Design: triple medallion pattern, pointed octagon design, simple medallion with stylized flower design and animal patterns.

Colours: blue, madder red or beige.

Sizes: rugs and up to 5 ft. 10 in. × 8 ft. 4 in. approx. (175 × 250 cm.).

Density: 77-194 knots per sq. in. approx. (12-30 knots per sq. cm.).

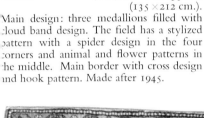

Derbent   4 ft. 5 in. × 7 ft. approx.
(135 × 212 cm.).

Main design: three medallions filled with cloud band design. The field has a stylized pattern with a spider design in the four corners and animal and flower patterns in the middle. Main border with cross design and hook pattern. Made after 1945.

Turkestan

Turkestan with East Turkestan, Afghanistan and Baluchistan

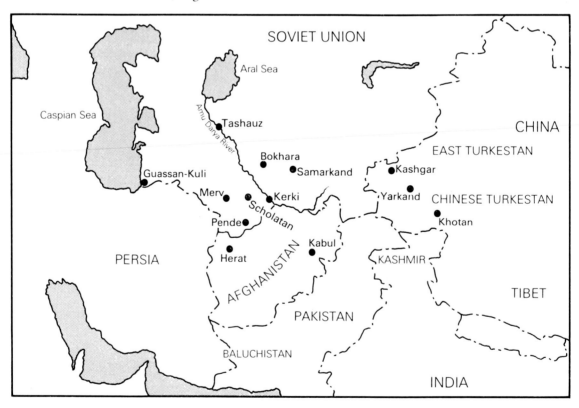

Turkestan extends over a wide area of Central Asia from the Caspian Sea into north-western China. Politically the area is now divided into the Soviet Republics of Turkmen, Usbek, Tadzhik and Kirgiz (West Turkestan) and the Sinkiang Uighur Autonomous Region of China (East Turkestan).

Turkoman carpet-making enjoyed a prolonged golden age from the second half of the 14th century under the celebrated conqueror Timur the Lame, who was a great patron of science, architecture, trade and the applied arts. Descendants of Timur made Herat in Afghanistan their residence and this became famous for the skill of its craftsmen, its gold and silver work and perhaps above all for its carpets, which were praised for their beauty by Marco Polo.

Regular exports of Turkoman carpets to Europe and America did not start until the end of the 19th century.

The Turkoman districts best known for their carpets today are Ashkabad, Bakharden, Guassan-Kuli, Gueok-Tepe, Kerki, Kizil-Arvat, Merv, Tadgen and Tashauz.

Tekke and Salor carpets are also made in northeast Persia where the Turkoman weaving technique has been inherited from the craftsmen who were called in from Merv in the 18th century.

The carpets of East Turkestan have Chinese patterns and colours. East Turkestan was renamed Sinkiang ("the new dominion") when the Chinese regained control in 1877. It was incorporated in Communist China in 1943.

Only the strips of country along the major rivers can be cultivated and most of the 212,360 square miles (550,000 sq. km.) is made up of mountains and sterile deserts. The sand dunes of the Takla-Makan desert are steadily encroaching on new areas. In the mountains there are wild donkeys and wild sheep and goats; in the desert areas wild horses, camel and antelope. The major caravan route that crosses the Gobi desert has been improved and can now be used by motor vehicles.

Afghanistan is another country that has suffered many invasions and consequently has a large racial intermixture; the major ethnic group, the Afghans proper, is of Pathan origin. Conquered in turn by the Mongols and the Moguls, Afghanistan in the 19th century had to fight off British encroachment; its independence was finally recognized in 1921. Since 1930 the country has been a constitutional monarchy under the Amir.

The Afghans, related to the peoples of Persia, Pakistan and north-west India, are orthodox Mos-

Afghan   3 ft. 8 in. × 5 ft. 3 in. approx.
(112 × 160 cm.).
Main design: three octagons and a floral
zig-zag design around the edges. Main
border: floral design. Made after 1945.

lems, but their women are freer than is customary among Mohammedan people and those of the higher classes are able to obtain a good education.

Baluchistan, a region that extends across southeast Persia and the south of Pakistan, is geologically a continuation of the Iranian mountains, with lofty mountain ranges and curious eroded formations. The country is of little economic importance, though in the lowlands the gardens provide delicious fruit when the rainfall is sufficient: almonds, olives, peaches, and figs. The Baluchi, who entered the country in the 13th century, are nomadic by nature but are gradually though unwillingly turning into farmers. The Brahui, the largest ethnic group after the Baluchi, make a living, as do the other nomadic tribes, from their herds in the mountains, where they follow their sheep and goats from pasture to pasture. The camel is still the normal method of transport. More than 90 per cent of the inhabitants are orthodox Moslems.

Baluchi carpets are largely made by the nomadic herdsmen during their wanderings along the eastern boundary of Persia up towards Meshed or over the western boundary of Afghanistan and up towards Herat.

The carpet districts in this section are arranged as follows:

Turkestan:
Yomud
Beshir
Hatchlou (Enessi)
Ersari
Saryk-Bokhara
Tekke
Kizil-Ajak
Salor
Tschoval
Jolam

Baluchistan:

East Turkestan:
Samarkand
Khotan
Kashgar
Yarkand

Afghanistan:

144

Yomud   6 ft. 3 in. ×9 ft. 4 in. approx.
                          (190 × 285 cm.).
Main design: diamond design with hook
pattern. Main border: small stylized floral
border surrounded by "S" guards. Made
after 1945.

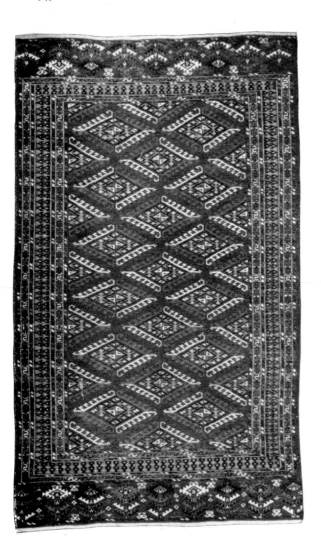

YOMUD

Made in: Guassan-Kuli and Tashauz in Western
Turkestan near the Caspian Sea. Nomad carpets.
Knot: Ghiordes or Sehna.
Warp: wool.
Weft: wool and goats' hair, 2 shoots after each row
of knots.
Pile: wool.
Fringe: wide, multi-coloured woven edge with
ordinary or braided fringe at either end.
Design: geometrical diamond design, often with
hooked edges, the border pattern at the ends being
different from those along the sides. Newer carpets
have Tekke-like octagons (see page 151), though
they are more squarely drawn.
Colours: reddish brown and dark violet with harsher
shades than those in the Tekke carpets.
Sizes: anything up to 8 ft. 4 in. × 13 ft. 4 in. approx.
(250 × 400 cm.).
Density: 58-309 knots per sq. in. approx. (9-48 knots
per sq. cm.).

    The selvages are made in different ways. Newer
carpets are oversewn in one colour, but older ones
have a two- or three-stringed weave, either in a dark
colour or with a square pattern in dark blue and
red. As a rule the Yomud carpets feel somewhat
coarser and have rougher colours than the various
Bokhara types made elsewhere in Turkestan.

BESHIR

Made in: the city of Beshir and the surrounding district along the river Amu Darya; the population is partly settled and partly semi-nomadic.

Knot: Sehna.

Warp: wool and goats' hair.

Weft: wool and goats' hair, 2 shoots after each row of knots.

Pile: heavy wool.

Fringe: broad, multi-coloured, woven edge with ordinary fringe at either end.

Design: three different groups of patterns.

1. One to five geometric medallions, usually three.
2. Guerat pattern, highly stylized flower design, covering the entire field.
3. Ilan pattern, stylized design resembling cloud band with surrounding small geometric design covering the entire carpet. These carpets differ from others made in Turkestan in that they are dominated by the pattern, whereas in the others the ground colour predominates.

Colours: brick-red ground with clear yellow, green and blue colours in the patterns.

Sizes: rugs and up to 10 ft.×16 ft. 8 in. approx. (300×500 cm.).

Density: 58-161 knots per sq. in. approx. (9-25 knots per sq. cm.).

The Beshir carpet resembles the Ersari and Afghan but may be distinguished by the clear brick-red colours, the more massive quality and greater stability, as well as by its much rougher feel. Production includes some very interesting prayer rugs with Mihrab design.

Beshir (prayer rug)
3 ft. 9 in. × 5 ft. 11 in. approx. (115 × 180 cm.).
Main design: three prayer niches with different patterns. Main border: rosette pattern. Made about 1880.

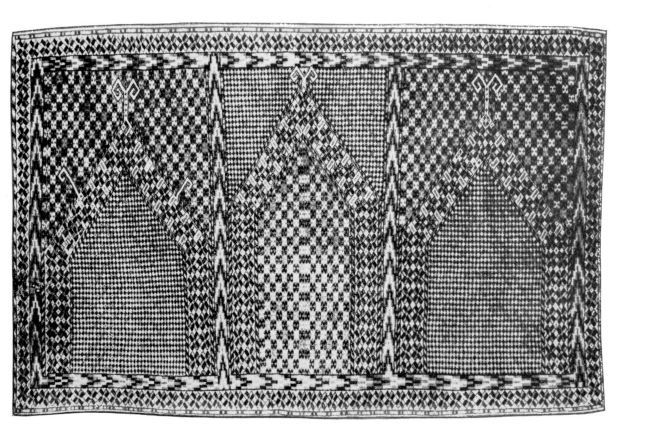

HATCHLOU (Enessi)

Made in: the whole of Central Asia.

Knot: Sehna.

Warp: wool and goats' hair.

Weft: wool and goats' hair, 2 shoots after each row of knots.

Pile: wool.

Fringe: dyed, woven edge and fringe at one end; the other end has a hemmed edge with thin plaited ropes for hanging up the carpet.

Design: cross-like design dividing the carpet into four parts, the fields of which have various types of candlestick designs. The borders at the end are different, the lower and wider one having an Avadan or Kabyrga border resembling the end borders of Yomud carpets.

Colours: red shades that vary with the district.

Hatchlou-Afghan 4 ft. 5 in. × 7 ft. 2 in. approx. (135 × 220 cm.).
Main design: cross-like pattern dividing the carpet into four parts, the fields of which have a design resembling candlesticks. Border: outer guard, double hook design; main border, diamonds and double hook design; in the other guards, a carnation design.

Ersari 6 ft. 10 in. × 9 ft. 2 in. approx. (207 × 280 cm.).
Main design: octagon design and cross design with hook pattern. The dog pattern inside the octagons is typical of the carpets from this area. Main border: diamonds with hook pattern along each end, wavy hook pattern down the sides.

ERSARI

Made in: the valley district of the river Amu Darya in Bokhara. Semi-nomads and settled peoples of Mongolian origin.

Knot: Sehna.

Warp: wool and goats' hair.

Weft: wool and goats' hair, 2 shoots after each row of knots.

Pile: heavy wool.

Fringe: wide, multi-coloured, woven edge with ordinary fringe at either end.

Design: octagon design resembling the Afghan pieces, usually with a dog design inside the octagon; sometimes the smaller octagons of the Tekke carpets are also used.

Colours: red or brown-red.

Sizes: rugs and up to 10 ft. × 13 ft. 4 in. approx. (300 × 400 cm.).

Density: 58-161 knots per sq. in. approx. (9-25 knots per sq. cm.).

Sizes: Tekke and similar qualities up to 4 ft. 7 in. × 6 ft. 8 in. approx. (140 × 200 cm.). Afghan and similar up to 6 ft. 8 in. × 9 ft. 2 in. approx. (200 × 275 cm.).

Density: Tekke 129-645 knots per sq. in. (20-100 knots per sq. cm.). Afghan 58-232 knots per sq. in. (9-36 knots per sq. cm.).

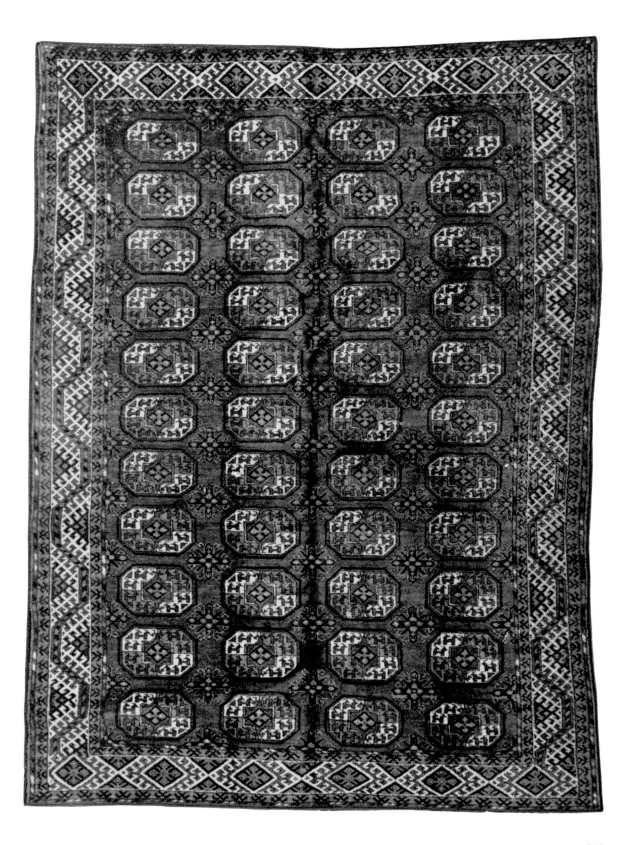

149

Saryk   3 ft. 9 in. × 5 ft. 5 in. approx.
(115 × 165 cm.).
Main design: a number of rectilinear octagons. Main border: highly stylized flower and star design. Made in the 1930s.

Tekke   3 ft. 7 in. × 6 ft. 1 in. approx.
(110 × 185 cm.).
Main design: three rows of ordinary octagons with diamonds in between. Main border: small star octagons with spider design. Made in the 1930s.

TEKKE

Made in: chiefly the city of Merv but also in Akhal, Mouri, Bakharden, Gueok-Tepe, Kizil-Arvat, Tadgen and Ashkabad, towards the Caspian Sea.
Knot: Sehna.
Warp: wool.
Weft: wool or goats' hair, 2 shoots after each row of knots.
Pile: fine quality wool.
Fringe: narrow, woven edge and ordinary or braided fringe at either end.
Design: graceful octagon design, known as Gul, and spider design to fill in. The main border has smaller octagons or spider design.
Colours: light copper or wine red.
Sizes: anything up to 13 ft. 2 in. × 16 ft. 5 in. approx. (400 × 500 cm.) and Enessi.
Density: 129-645 knots per sq. in. approx. (20-100 knots or more per sq. cm.).

The Tekke tribe is the largest in Turkestan. The nomads only make rugs; the larger carpets are made in the towns.

SARYK-BOKHARA

Made by: nomads in the district of Scholatan and the Pende oases in southern Turkestan.
Knot: Sehna.
Warp: wool.
Weft: wool or goats' hair, 2 shoots after each row of knots.
Pile: heavy wool.
Fringe: narrow woven edge and ordinary fringe at either end.
Design: geometrical oblong octagons, often containing a dog design with the field filled in with smaller octagons or spider patterns.
Colours: terracotta red or reddish-brown ground with dark patterns in blue and yellow ochre.

Sizes: rugs and Enessi, i.e., tent-door hangings, known in the trade as Hatchlou.
Density: 103-363 knots per sq. in. approx. (16-56 knots per sq. cm.).

Enessi, tent-door carpets, are made everywhere in Turkestan and consequently are available in all qualities. The Saryk carpets are sometimes known as Pende or Kizil-Ajak, though this is wrong. It is difficult to distinguish this carpet from its closest relation, Salor, but the Saryk is somewhat coarser and has browner shades of colour than those found in the Salor carpets. There are also certain differences in the pattern. The Saryk octagon has straighter lines and its spider pattern is simpler in the rays.

151

KIZIL-AJAK

Made in: a community approximately 25 miles (40 km.) from the city of Kerki. Nomad carpets.

Knot: Sehna.

Warp: wool and goats' hair.

Weft: wool and goats' hair, 2 shoots after each row of knots.

Pile: heavy wool.

Fringe: wide, coloured woven edge with ordinary fringe at either end.

Design: two types of octagons, a stepped one with secondary diamond design and oblong octagons reminiscent of the Ersari octagons and with smaller secondary designs, also very like the Afghan carpets.

Colours: brown or brick-red.

Sizes: rugs and up to 8 ft. 4 in. × 13 ft. 4 in. approx. (250 × 400 cm.).

Density: 58-129 knots per sq. in. approx. (9-20 knots per sq. cm.).

This type of carpet is very difficult to assess and is often confused with ordinary Afghan carpets. A characteristic is that the secondary pattern in the field is repeated as a pattern in the main border.

Kizil-Ajak   5 ft. 11 in. × 11 ft. 4 in. approx.
(180 × 345 cm.).
Main design: simple octagon design with ray-shaped spider design. Main border: spider design. Made after 1930.

SALOR

Made by: nomads in the district of Serak, Pende and Tejend oases, close to the border with Persia.

Knot: Sehna.

Warp: wool.

Weft: wool or goats' hair, 2 shoots after each row of knots.

Pile: fine quality wool.

Fringe: narrow, woven edge and ordinary fringe at either end.

Design: geometrical octagons with spiked outer edges as the main design and with smaller stepped octagons to fill in with, all the octagons arranged in rows.

Colours: dark mahogany or blue-red.

Sizes: rugs and up to 10 ft. × 20 ft. approx. (300 × 600 cm.).

Density: 129-516 knots per sq. in. approx. (20-80 knots per sq. cm.).

In public trade these carpets are known as Bokhara, or Bokhara preceded by either Royal, Princess, Pende or Pendic. The first two terms are used to indicate a higher quality. However, their use varies considerably and cannot always be relied on. Salor is considered to be one of the best types of Turkestan carpet.

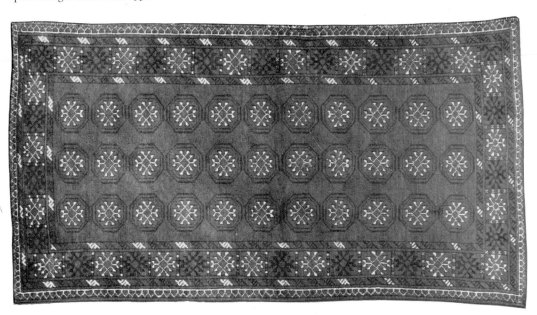

Salor   5 ft. 8 in. ×
         9 ft. approx.
(173 × 275 cm.).
Main design: three
rows of rectilinear
octagons. Main
border: Mir–Ibotha
pattern on blue
background. Made
in the 1920s.

TSCHOVAL (camel bag)

Made in: the whole of Turkestan.
Knot: Sehna, occasionally Ghiordes.
Warp: wool.
Weft: wool, 2 shoots after each row of knots.
Pile: heavy wool.
Fringe: as a rule both ends are hemmed to the open-weave back of the bag.
Design: the customary octagon design of the district or small geometric patterns. The border along the lower edge differs from the rest.
Colours: different shades of red.

Sizes: 2 ft.-3 ft. 4 in. × 3 ft. 11 in.-5 ft. 11 in. approx. (60-100 × 120-180 cm.).
Density: 77-406 knots per sq. in. approx. (12-63 knots per sq. cm.).

The names for camel bags and storage bags vary from country to country as do the names for the different sizes (see lists, pages 213-214). Those made in Persia and Turkey are usually small and are called Churdjin. In the Caucasus the name for large ones is Mafrash, while in Turkestan it is Tschoval and the smaller ones are known as Torba. All the names are frequently used in one and the same country.

Tschoval (camel bag)
2 ft. 7 in. × 5 ft. 1 in. approx.
(82 × 155 cm.).
The front of a large saddle bag; popularly known as a camel bag. Main design: typical Yomud octagons. Main border with cross design, surrounded by two guards with reciprocal "running dog" design. Made in the 1920s.

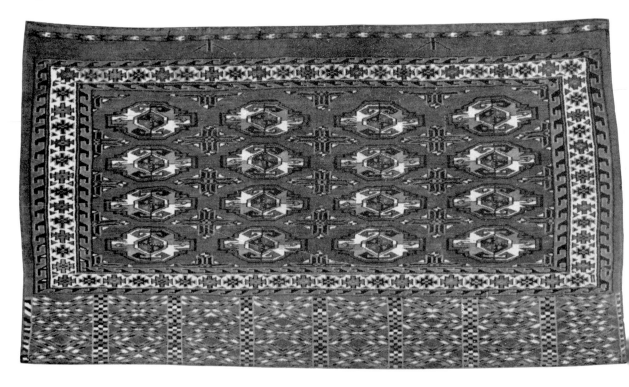

JOLAM

Made in: Turkestan.
Knot: Sehna.
Warp: wool.
Weft: wool and linen. The weft forms a base that is more visible than in ordinary carpets.
Pile: fine-spun wool.
Fringe: wide patterned edge and braided or plaited fringe.
Design: tree and other stylized small design.

Colours: predominantly red but blue and golden yellow also occur.
Sizes: 10 in.-1 ft. 4 in. × 11-17 yards approx. (25-40 cm. × 10-15 m.).
Density: 161-258 knots per sq. in. approx. (25-40 knots per sq. cm.).

The technique for these pieces is generally relief with the dark details knotted and the intervening plain ground (the weft) woven. Used to decorate the tent.

Jolam 1 ft. 1 in. × 49 ft. 10 in. approx. (32 × 1,520 cm.).
These bands hang as an ornamental frieze on the walls of the primitive, tent-like dwellings known as Kibitka. The bands are made in relief, with the dark parts and the pattern knotted on to the smoothly woven light ground.

Baluchi 3 ft. 5 in. ×6 ft. 3 in. approx.
(105 × 190 cm.).
Main design: niche and tree of life design.
Border: rectilinear stylized design. Made
after 1945.

BALUCHISTAN

Made by: nomads who wander from the Arabian
sea along the Persian borders up towards Meshed
or into Afghanistan towards Herat.

Knot: Sehna.

Warp: wool.

Weft: wool and goats' hair, 2 shoots after each row
of knots.

Pile: wool.

Fringe: sometimes artistically woven edge and
braided or ordinary fringe at either end.

Design: very varied octagon, diamond, spider,
Mina-Khani, star, niche and tree of life designs.

Colours: red, blue; beige or brown ground and
sometimes an effective lustrous white, bleached wool.

Sizes: mostly rugs but also Kellei up to 5 ft. 7 in. ×
11 ft. 8 in. approx. (170×350 cm.).

Density: Meshed-Baluchi 58-309 knots per sq. in.
approx. (9-48 knots per sq. cm.). Herat-Baluchi
58-161 knots per sq. in. approx. (9-25 knots per sq.
cm.).

There are two types of Baluchistan, the better or
Meshed-Baluchi and the simpler, known as Herat-
Baluchi or Arabi-Baluchi.

SAMARKAND

Made in: East Turkestan.

Knot: Sehna.

Warp: cotton.

Weft: cotton, 4 shoots after each row of knots.

Pile: wool, occasionally silk.

Fringe: narrow, woven edge and braided fringe at either end.

Design: Chinese influence, 1-3 large medallions surrounded by smaller, similar medallion designs, highly stylized motifs such as porcelain and clay vessels, tables and similar household articles.

Colours: hard, glaring colours with violet, blue or yellow ground; older carpets have somewhat milder shades.

Sizes: rugs and up to 8 ft. 2 in. × 16 ft. 5 in. approx. (250 × 500 cm.).

Density: 58-236 knots per sq. in. approx. (9-35 knots per sq. cm.).

Samarkand is a collective name for carpets manufactured in Kashgar, Yarkand and Khotan and the neighbouring districts. No carpets are produced in Samarkand itself. This collective name has been used at all times owing to the difficulty of determining exactly where the carpets have been made. Bokhara is another collective name of this type. Most of the Samarkand carpets generally come from Yarkand.

Samarkand   4 ft. 2 in. × 5 ft. 6 in. approx (129 × 168 cm.).
Main design: vase and tree design with pomegranate and flower pattern. Main border with wavy band design. Made in the 1930s.

KHOTAN, KASHGAR
AND YARKAND

Made in: Chinese Turkestan.

Knot: Sehna.

Warp: cotton or silk.

Weft: cotton, 2-4 shoots after each row of knots.

Pile: heavy wool, also silk.

Fringe: narrow, woven edge and braided fringe at either end.

Design: ancient Chinese geometrical pattern and coarsely stylized flower design, octagon, animal, dragon and other typically Chinese small designs.

Colours: Chinese blue, beige, yellow and violet-red.

Sizes: rugs and up to 8 ft. 9 in. × 16 ft. 5 in. approx. (270 × 500 cm.).

Density: Khotan 58-161 knots per sq. in. approx. (9-25 knots per sq. cm.).
Kashgar 58-236 knots per sq. in. approx. (9-35 knots per sq. cm.).
Yarkand 58-236 knots per sq. in. approx. (9-35 knots per sq. cm.).

Kashgar   3 ft. 1 in. × 5 ft. 9 in. approx.
                (94 × 175 cm.).
Main design: double vases with flower design, two large pomegranates and, on either side of the centre, two hour-glass designs. Main border: swastika pattern. Made in the 1920s.

Silk-Khotan   4 ft. 4 in. × 7 ft. approx.
                    (132 × 213 cm.).
Main design: items from among the "hundred antiquities" surrounded by Shou border. Main border with tree peony, cherry flower and bamboo design. From the 1930s.

159

Afghan   3 ft. 11 in. × 5 ft. 3 in. approx.
                       (120 × 160 cm.).
Main design: three characteristic guls
supplemented by V-shaped hook design.
Main border: triangle design. Made after
1945.

AFGHANISTAN

Made in: northern Afghanistan, by nomads and
settled tribes.
Knot: Sehna.
Warp: wool and goats' hair.
Weft: wool and goats' hair, 2 shoots after each row
of knots.
Pile: wool of varying quality.
Fringe: dyed, woven edge and ordinary fringe at
either end.
Design: large and small octagons and diamond
designs filled in with spider design and other geo-
metrically stylized details.
Colours: all shades of red.
Sizes: anything up to 13 ft. 2 in. × 20 ft. approx.
(400 × 600 cm.).
Density: 58-232 knots per sq. in. approx. (9-36 knots
per sq. cm.).

The Afghan carpet is one of the most popular
today, partly because it is relatively cheap but also
because its patterns are so simple and calm. The red
colour with its dominating plain ground makes
these carpets easy to place even in a modern home.
There are many qualities with large differences in
density and the quality of the wool. There are also
"golden Afghans", most of which were originally
red but have been specially washed and bleached to
produce their bronze-yellow colour. This can be
checked by inspecting the base of the pile.

China

Districts and places in China where carpets are made.

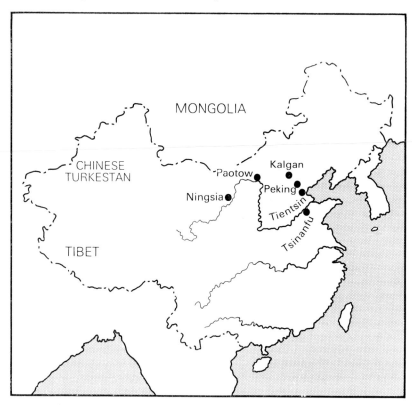

Ancient Chinese documents confirm that carpets were being made in China two thousand years ago, under the Han dynasty at the time of the birth of Christ. However, production seems to have been largely confined to supplying the imperial court.

The ordinary Chinaman knew nothing about woven carpets. The Chinese mostly lived a settled life and managed with simple carpets of straw. The nomadic Chinese contented themselves with un-coloured carpets of woollen felt.

In China it was only the houses of princes and the magnificent palaces of the rich that had woven carpets of wool or silk.

Carpets do not seem to have been regularly woven until late in the Ming dynasty. Chien-lung (1736-96), one of China's most distinguished rulers and a great patron of the arts, may have encouraged their production, since the earliest surviving carpets date from his reign.

The provinces or former provinces with an ancient tradition of carpet-making are Kansu, Ningsia and Suiyuan. Later came Shansi, Chili (Hopeh) and Shantung, where manufacturing is now highly organized.

The materials are always the same but the qualities vary somewhat.

The difference in quality within each group is chiefly due to the density—80, 90, 100 or 110 knots per foot (30 cm.) laterally—and to whether the warp is single or double. While a double warp requires more wool, the carpet will be much more durable.

The depth of the pile varies according to the principle 1 cm., 1.2 cm., 1.5 cm. The most closely knotted carpets with the longest pile are the most expensive but also represent the best quality.

The carpets being produced today are made of machine-spun wool, coloured with fast chemical dyes and with the warp and weft of machine-spun cotton.

The knot is the Sehna. The patterns are quite different in type from other oriental carpet patterns and have been derived from domestic handicrafts—from the silk weavers and the porcelain painters as well as from ancient Chinese symbols, both religious and profane.

The types of patterns used during the various dynasties are as follows:

Ming 1368-1644
Geometrical arabesques and animal designs, medallion and corners as well as symbolic designs.
Kang-hsi 1662-1722
The softer outlines of the Ming period's patterns are further accentuated.
Chien-lung 1736-96
Largely the same as the above, though with the addition of everyday attributes, the "hundred antiquities": tables, books, butterflies, bats, birds, cases and vases.
Chia-ching 1796-1820
Flower design, Buddha's dog, dragons, meander design, the Shou sign, swastika and T border.
Tao-kuang 1820-50
All the patterns were used during this period. The tendency was to make the patterns larger and to accentuate the outline.

More recent production, which comprises more than 300 patterns, can be grouped as follows:
Tun-Huang patterns
Motifs from the ancient burial caves with delicately drawn flower designs, arranged as medallions and border. The colours are pale, usually matching. Relief trimmed (where the outlines are clipped so that each motif stands out).
Flower patterns
Relief trimmed, matching or colourful motifs with flower bouquets or bunches, arranged diagonally or simply in the form of flower borders with a completely plain field.
Style patterns
European patterns with oblong medallions and broken floral borders. Relief trimmed, wide colour scale.

Matching relief
Flower patterned medallion or diagonal design. The pattern in these lies about one centimetre above the ground which was trimmed shorter while the carpet was still being made.
Oriental patterns
Geometrical Herati, medallion and octagon designs are copied. This type is manufactured on a relatively small scale and since the difference in structure from the original is considerable, these patterns have little to justify them.

Formerly, certain patterns and symbols were reserved for imperial or religious work and could not be used for anything else. Thus the five-clawed dragon was reserved for the emperor and the reddish-yellow colour for the mandarins.

Symbols for different religions could not be mixed in one and the same carpet. With the coming of the republic the feeling and respect for this attitude gradually disappeared—if anyone desires, he may now order a carpet with the imperial dragon and religious symbols mixed in any design he likes. But the main thing is that even modern carpets can be made with patterns that go back a thousand years and in the most varied colours.

The best known symbols are described on pages 42-43.

Since it is not possible to differentiate between the production of different districts, only the districts from which carpets are now available will be dealt with here.

Older type	Newer type
Ningsia	Tientsin
Paotow	Peking
Peking (Northern China)	Tsinanfu
	Kalgan

Northern China

6 ft. 3 in. ×6 ft. 5 in. approx.
(190 × 195 cm.).
Main design: five imperial five-clawed
dragons and cloud band. Main border:
swastika border. Made about 1890.

168

NINGSIA (old type)

Made in: the former province of Ningsia in north-west China.

Knot: Sehna.

Warp: finely spun cotton.

Weft: cotton, 2-4 shoots after each row of knots.

Pile: heavy wool.

Fringe: very narrow, woven edge with ordinary fringe on two sides.

Design: usually landscape and animal design, also repeating small, geometrical patterns. The pattern is often arranged to be viewed from one of the carpet's long sides. Relief trimmed.

Colours: blue, red or beige.

Sizes: rugs and up to 5 ft. 11 in. × 9 ft. 6 in. approx. (180 × 290 cm.).

Density: 77-161 knots per sq. in. approx. (12-25 knots per sq. cm.).

Ningsia   4 ft. 5 in. × 6 ft. 1 in. approx.
                          (135 × 185 cm.).
Main design: the crane and deer, mountain and lake design. Main border: diagonal swastika border. Made at the turn of the century.

PAOTOW (old type)

Made in: the city of Paotow in the province of Suiyuan.

Knot: Sehna.

Warp: finely spun cotton.

Weft: cotton, 2-4 shoots after each row of knots.

Pile: heavy wool.

Fringe: narrow, woven edge and ordinary fringe on two sides.

Design: landscape design like Ningsia, symbol design. These carpets are not relief trimmed and are generally of a finer quality than Ningsia.

Colours: blue, red, brown and beige.

Sizes: anything up to 11 ft. 8 in. × 19 ft. 2 in. approx. (350 × 575 cm.).

Density: 77-194 knots per sq. in. approx. (12-30 knots per sq. cm.).

Paotow   4 ft. 4 in. × 6 ft. 7 in. approx.
                                      (132 × 201 cm.).
Main design: patterns from the "hundred antiquities", the knot of destiny in each corner. Main border: peony and labyrinth border. Made around the turn of the century.

Main design: the imperial dragon, under this a wave pattern and to the right of the dragon's head the symbol of fire. Above and below the dragon a butterfly pattern. Main border with tree peony and prunus flower pattern. Made after 1950. Left: the dragon pattern in detail.

TIENTSIN

Made in: the city of Tientsin in the province of Hopeh.

Knot: Sehna.

Warp: cotton.

Weft: cotton, 2 shoots after each row of knots.

Pile: wool of varying depth.

Fringe: narrow, woven edge and braided or ordinary fringe at either end.

Design: all China's own patterns, French Aubusson and Savonnerie patterns and recently Persian and Turkoman patterns as well. Tientsin carpets are very carefully made and give the impression of being produced by machine in that the rows of knots are extremely even and straight; however, this is because the looms have a batten that extends right across the carpet, so that each row of knots receives the same even beating.

Colours: every colour imaginable.

Sizes: anything up to huge pieces.

Density: 58-103 knots per sq. in. approx. (9-16 knots per sq. cm.).

The carpets are generally relief trimmed or have a high relief because the ground was trimmed shorter during production. Tientsin has the highest production and export in the whole of China.

Peking   8 ft. × 10 ft. approx.
                          (244 × 305 cm.).
Main design: medallions with the round
Shou sign surrounded by bats (i.e., signs
of happiness only). Main border: the oblong
Shou sign; the innermost guard is a pearl
border, the next a "T" border. Made after
1945.

PEKING, TSINANFU AND KALGAN

Made in: the cities of Peking, Tsinanfu and Kalgan
in the provinces of Hopeh and Shansi.
Knot: Sehna.
Warp: cotton.
Weft: cotton, 2-4 shoots after each row of knots.
Pile: wool of varying depth.
Fringe: narrow, woven edge and braided or ordinary
fringe at either end.
Design: the older carpets have large dragon designs,
medallion and symbol designs executed in the
traditional manner. Production is now more organized and recent pieces have every imaginable
pattern and combination. Sometimes the outer
edges of the carpets are knotted with the Ghiordes
knot, since the tighter hold of this gives better
stability and resistance. Relief trimmed.
Colours: blue, yellow, green, red, pink and beige.
Sizes: anything up to huge pieces.
Density: 58-103 knots per sq. in. approx. (9-16
knots per sq. cm.).

In the Peking district a quality of carpet is also
manufactured that is different from the ordinary
production in that the pile is lower and the carpet
is made somewhat more loosely. The pattern is
always of an older type.

India
and Pakistan

India and Pakistan. Places and districts of manufacture.

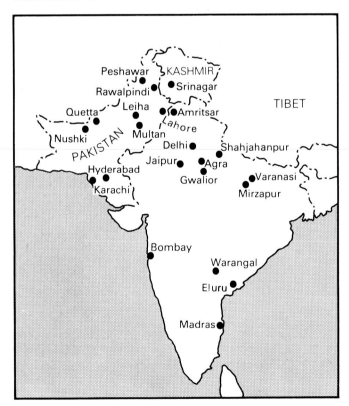

India and Pakistan became separate states only in 1947; thus, an account of the origin and development of carpet-weaving in the Indian sub-continent will serve for both countries. The designs used are mainly those of other oriental countries, and this section of the book has been arranged somewhat differently from the rest. Centres of carpet-making, in India and Pakistan respectively, are listed, but only the most important details of each type are given.

The organized manufacture of hand-knotted carpets began in the 16th century, when the Mogul emperor Akbar introduced from Persia skilled weavers and designers, who were initially employed in his own palace. The early Indian carpets, made of silk and fine wool, with Persian designs, were of very high quality; a number survive, and can be seen in museums, notably at Jaipur in India, and also in Europe and North America.

In the early period the centres of manufacture were Agra, Lahore, Delhi, Srinagar and Amritsar. Eventually carpet-making spread throughout the sub-continent. The Persian Sehna knot was used, and the warp was almost always of cotton or silk. The designs were mainly Persian, imitating the Isfahan, Kashan and Kerman types; the Herati pattern was also much used.

From the early 18th century both quality and technique deteriorated ; materials were inferior and weaving very coarse. But recently production has become more organized and has considerably increased; quality has also been improved.

In India, which, after Persia, exports the largest number of hand-knotted carpets, the leading area for production of fine quality carpets is now Kashmir, especially in and around the town of Srinagar. The northern wool used is of good quality, and excellent carpets, with high density knotting, are produced. The patterns are the imitation Persian ones already mentioned; some Turkoman, Chinese and Turkish designs have also recently been adopted. Where a distinctive Indian style has developed, as at Jaipur, it is characterized by naturalistic rather than

stylized treatment of floral and bird motifs. Ovals and loops are also used.

In Pakistan extremely tightly-woven carpets are now being made, some with more than 650 knots per sq. in. (100 per sq. cm.). The main centres of production are Lahore, Karachi and Rawalpindi.

Pakistan now includes part of Baluchistan, but the carpets from that region are described with those of Turkestan.

India

AGRA

Agra has long been a centre of carpet-making. Modern production is of two main types. In the first, carpets made to Persian or Turkoman patterns have densities of 95-400 knots per sq. in. (15-60 per sq. cm.). The second type, with either Chinese or French Savonnerie designs, have only 16-60 knots per sq. in. (2.5-9 per sq. cm.), but their coarseness is offset by an embossed effect, achieved by clipping round the outlines of the patterns.

AMRITSAR

Amritsar, with a long history of carpet-production, became a leading centre in the mid-19th century. Modern output is of good quality carpets with a variety of types of wool and density grades. Designs are mostly of Persian origin, but Turkestan Bokhara patterns have also been adopted.

BHADOHI

Fine carpets have been woven at Bhadohi since the 16th century. Modern production is mainly of carpets with densities of 60-100 knots per sq. in. (9-16 per sq. cm.), and mainly with Chinese or French Savonnerie designs. Bhadohi, with the neighbouring districts of Mirzapur and Varanasi, forms one of the major centres of India's carpet export industry.

Hyderabad   4 ft. 5 in. ×7 ft. 8 in. approx.
(135×236 cm.).
Main pattern: small and large arabesque design and a very dominating rosette design in white contrasting with the red ground (of silk). Main border: palmette and rosette design. The innermost guard is reciprocal, the white guards have a rosette and leaf design. Made early in the 19th century.

ELURU

Although very fine carpets, with Persian designs, were produced at Eluru in the 17th and 18th centuries, subsequent production has been of poor quality goods, with densities of only 13-32 knots per sq. in. (2-5 per sq. cm.). Very recently there has been some improvement.

JAIPUR

Jaipur has produced carpets since the 17th century. Modern production covers a wide range of qualities, the designs mainly Persian, although occasionally Turkoman or Chinese. Particularly notable is the Barjasta type, where the main design (usually animal and tree motifs) is knotted in relief over a flat-woven gold or silver thread field.

MIRZAPUR

A carpet-making centre from the 17th century, the Mirzapur district produces carpets of widely differing quality. The majority have densities of 26-60 knots per sq. in. (4-9 per sq. cm.), usually dyed in pastel shades. Recently, finer quality carpets, of 100-150 knots per sq. in. (16-24 per sq. cm.), have also been made. The designs are Persian, French Savonnerie and Chinese. A feature of Mirzapur production is the use of special looms on which carpets as wide as 40 ft. approx. (12 metres) can be made.

SHAHJAHANPUR

In Shahjahanpur about 500 families make carpets in their homes. The carpets are usually rather coarse, although densities of 26-40 knots per sq. in. (4-6 per sq. cm.) are sometimes achieved. The designs are simple geometric shapes.

SRINAGAR AND KASHMIR

Srinagar, capital of the state of Jammu and Kashmir, is the centre of the Kashmiri carpet-weaving industry. The local wool is of excellent quality, and high density carpets are produced, usually of ratios of 120-520 knots per sq. in. (19-80 per sq. cm.). The designs are mainly Persian and Turkoman, but sometimes Turkish, especially in Srinagar itself, where Turkish prayer rug motifs are copied. Srinagar also produces some carpets in which both pile and warp are of silk, and some in which part of the design is knotted in silk.

VARANASI

The carpets produced at Varanasi (formerly Benares) are similar to those of Bhadohi and Mirzapur, with which it is closely associated in the industry.

WARANGAL

Carpets made at Warangal in the 16th century are known to have been of very high quality. But today production is small, with densities of only 6.5-29 per sq. in. (1-4.5 per sq. cm.). All are made in weavers' homes. Designs are Persian with strong Indian characteristics.

Pakistan

BAHAWALPUR

Bahawalpur, a town and province near the Indian border, produces rather small rugs, with densities of about 100-150 knots per sq. in. (16-24 per sq. cm.). Designs are mainly of the Turkestan Bokhara type, or featuring the Turkish prayer niche.

BANNU

Bannu, a town near the Afghan border and south-west of Rawalpindi, produces carpets of densities of around 100-190 knots per sq. in. (16-30 per sq. cm.). The most common designs are the Bokhara, used for rugs, and the Mori (similar to the Tekke patterns, but with slightly smaller octagons and paler colours), used for larger carpets of 6 ft. 6 in. ×9 ft. 10 in. approx. (about 200×300 cm.).

GUJAR-KHAN

At Gujar-Khan, a smallish town south of Rawalpindi, carpets of densities of about 100-150 knots per sq. in. (16-24 per sq. cm.) are made. Most are small, although a few are about 6 ft. 6 in.×9 ft. 10 in. (about 200×300 cm.). The designs are mainly Bokhara type, in a variety of colours; a few are Turkish.

HYDERABAD

At Hyderabad, a town north-east of Karachi, carpets of densities of 60-190 knots per sq. in. (9-30 per sq. cm.) are made, and all sizes up to 8 ft. 2 in. × 11 ft. 6 in. approx. (250 × 350 cm.). The designs are usually Turkoman and Turkish, but latterly some Chinese have been introduced.

KARACHI

Karachi lies at the centre of one of Pakistan's major carpet-weaving districts. Densities cover a wide range, and some carpets have up to 650 knots per sq. in. (100 per sq. cm.). Production includes rugs, runners, and carpets up to 9 ft. 10 in. × 13 ft. (300 × 400 cm.), and even larger ones are made to order. The designs are mainly Bokhara type, but differ from those made in Turkestan in that the background, normally red, may in Karachi carpets be of almost any colour.

LAHORE

Lahore, where carpets were made from the 16th century, is now one of the largest centres of Pakistan's carpet industry. Normal densities vary between 100-390 knots per sq. in. (16-60 per sq. cm.), although some of up to 650 per sq. in. (100 per sq. cm.) can be found. Sizes vary from rugs and strips to carpets of 9 ft. 10 in. × 13 ft. (300 × 400 cm.); and larger ones may be specially ordered. The range of designs is extensive, including the Bokhara, Turkish prayer niche patterns, and Persian Kerman, Saruk, Tabriz and Isfahan types.

LEIHA

Leiha, a town north of Lahore, produces on a small scale rugs of 75-190 knots per sq. in. (12-30 per sq. cm.) in density and up to 5 ft. 3 in. × 8 ft. 2 in. approx. (160 × 250 cm.) in size. The designs are Bokhara, Mori, and the Turkish prayer niche.

MITHI

Mithi, a small town east of Karachi, produces carpets of densities of 75-190 knots per sq. in. (12-30 per sq. cm.) and of all sizes up to 6 ft. 6 in.×9 ft. 10 in. (200×300 cm.). The design is normally Bokhara type on a red or beige background.

MULTAN

Multan, south-west of Lahore, produces carpets of densities varying from about 60-190 knots per sq. in. (9-30 per sq. cm.), and of all sizes up to 8 ft. 2 in. × 11 ft. 6 in. approx. (250×350 cm.). The designs are Persian, Turkoman, Turkish and Chinese.

NUSHKI

At Nushki, near the Afghan border, and south of Quetta, the Baluchi and Afghan nomads trade their carpets (see under Turkestan). Local production, not extensive, is of small size rugs of densities of 60-150 knots per sq. in. (9-24 per sq. cm.), and of Bokhara, Baluchi and Afghan designs.

QUETTA

Like Nushki, Quetta is a centre where nomads sell their carpets. The local production is of small rugs with densities of about 60-150 knots per sq. in. (9-24 per sq. cm.), and the designs are Bokhara, Baluchi and Afghan.

RAWALPINDI

Rawalpindi's carpets are of densities of 60-260 knots per sq. in. (9-40 per sq. cm.). To the traditional range of Persian, Turkish, Afghan and Bokhara designs, Chinese styles have recently been added.

Woven Carpets

and Kelim

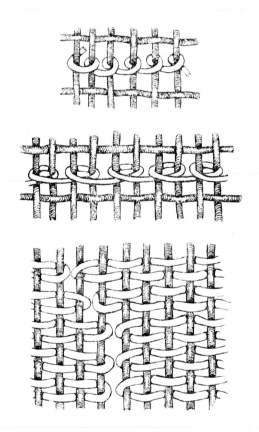

Sumakh technique. The pattern weft is taken around each warp thread.

Sumakh technique. The pattern weft is taken around every two warp threads.

Kelim technique. This shows how slits may be formed.

A number of interesting plain-woven carpets are produced in the Caucasus as well as in Turkestan on a smaller scale; the foremost types are Sumakh, Sille and Verne.

SUMAKH

The technique in this carpet is a sort of herring-bone weave, the pattern thread being looped round one or two warp threads at a time. The reverse of such a carpet looks rather like a hooked rug, with all the loose threads that are left hanging when the weaver starts with a new colour. The pattern in these carpets is always geometrical.

SILLE

This type is also woven with the Sumakh technique but has quite another design. This is nearly always a large geometrical "S" design, repeated in two colours all over the carpet.

VERNE

This carpet is made partly with the Sumakh technique but differs from the pure Sumakh in that the colours of the warp and weft threads are used for their effect between the "herring-bone" pattern. The pattern in these carpets is usually an enclosed bird design.

In the district of Merv in Turkestan a Sumakh type is woven with a small diamond design but the colours are much more sombre and less varied than in the Caucasian Sumakh carpet. In the trade it is known as Turkoman-Sumakh or Merv-Pallas. The latter name, however, is the ordinary term for Kelims from this district.

KELIM

Kelim weaving is regarded as an ancient home-craft of high artistic quality. Most homes only had small looms, so that a Kelim was usually woven in two or more parts with extremely accurate fitting of the pattern. Because of the technique, only geometrical patterns and narrow stripes are produced.

Kelims are made in Turkey, from where production has spread to the former Turkish parts of the Balkan peninsula, and also in the Caucasus,

Persia and Turkestan. The Turkish Kelim is known as Karaman; in the other countries the term Kelim is used.

Very few can be used as floor rugs and most are used for draperies and covers for ottomans and other furniture. A number of small Kelims are also woven; these are known as Kis-Kelim and are used as prayer rugs.

It is an oriental custom that the bride-to-be should weave a small carpet or Kelim for her future husband. Thanks to this custom one finds many wonderfully fine Kis-Kelims as proof of the wife-to-be's weaving skill.

Another well-known piece is the Sehna-Kelim. This type, the finest of all the Kelims, is made in western Persia and takes its name from the city of Sehna, now known as Sanandaj. It is generally woven with slits but with excellent, fine-spun yarn. The pattern is typical of the Sehna district with borders and often with a niche design. The very best pieces are woven without slits, using the ordinary Kelim technique.

Sehna-Kelim 4 ft. ×6 ft. 7 in. approx. (122 × 200 cm.). Main design: stepped diamond enclosing a smaller diamond; network with stylized flower design. The design of the field is the Herati pattern. Main border: rectilinear flower design.

Sille   6 ft. 7 in. × 11 ft. 3 in. approx.
(200 × 342 cm.).
Main design: four rows of six large, rectangular "S" designs; these are filled in with small reverse "S" designs. Made at the turn of the century.

SILLE

Made in: the district around Baku in the Caucasus.
Technique: herring-bone weave.
Warp: wool.
Weft: wool or cotton.
Pattern weave: wool.
Fringe: plaited or braided fringe at either end.
Pattern: large angular "S" design in alternate light and dark colour with small geometrical patterns in the wide "S" figure; geometrical fill-in designs between the main pattern.
Colours: blue or red.
Sizes: medium size and up to 7 ft. 8 in. × 13 ft. 2 in. approx. (235 × 400 cm.).
This type is usually woven in two parts with the patterns fitted so that both halves can be sewn together. The "S" design was originally a stylized dragon design.

Verne   4 ft. 3 in. × 6 ft. 1 in. approx.
(128 × 185 cm.).
Main design: lateral pattern with animal design, e.g., cocks, chickens and dogs. Main border: two borders with double hook pattern, also known as the double "T" design. Made in the 1920s.

VERNE

Made in: the Karabagh district in the southern Caucasus.
Technique: herring-bone weave and two and one twill weave.
Warp: dyed wool.
Weft: dyed wool.
Pattern weave: wool.
Fringe: plaited or braided fringe at either end.
Design: rectangular main pattern. Each rectangle is dominated by a bird and animal design as well as ordinary geometrical small designs, also stripes with animal and geometrical designs.
Colours: red or blue ground, the squares outlined in shades of light beige.
Sizes: medium sizes and up to 6 ft. 8 in. × 10 ft. approx. (200 × 300 cm.).
The Verne and Sille types are light, and Kelim-like; consequently they are not always suitable as floor carpets but make excellent draperies and couch covers.

Shirvan-Pallas   5 ft. 4 in. ×13 ft. 5 in.
approx. (162×410 cm.).
Main design: rectangles in different colours
with typical Caucasian flower and spider
designs. Border design: the same as the field
along the sides, other Caucasian designs at
each end. This particular Kelim has been
made in two parts with the patterns extremely well matched. Made around 1880.
Left: detail in colour.

SHIRVAN-PALLAS

Made in: the Caucasus.
Technique: Kelim weave with or without slits.
Warp: wool or goats' hair or a mixture of both.
Pattern weave: heavy wool, tightly spun.
Fringe: braided fringe at either end.
Pattern: geometrical pattern in stripes; usually
woven in one piece, sometimes in two.
Colours: dark but clear colours in red, blue, yellow
and beige.
Sizes: usually approx. 5 ft. 3 in.×8 ft. 11 in. (160×
275 cm.), but up to 7 ft. 9 in.×11 ft. 10 in. approx.
(240×360 cm.).

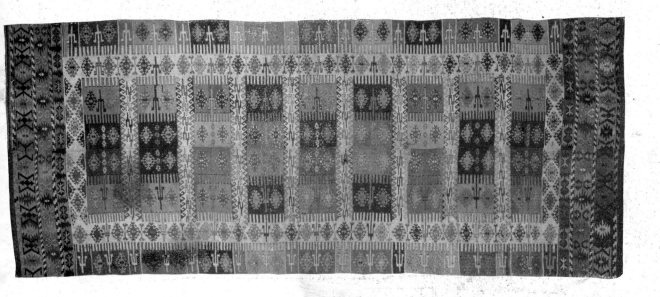

Sumakh
3 ft. 10 in. ×7 ft. 9 in. approx.
(118×240 cm.).
Main design: four hexagonal
medallions with stylized flower
design. Note the variation in the
colour of the background, due to
a discrepancy in dyeing (abrash).
Main border: stylized flower
design. Made at the turn of the
century.

Sumakh-Churdjin
1 ft. 8 in. × 3 ft. 11 in. approx.
(50 × 120 cm.).
The reverse of this saddle bag has the same appearance as the section between the decorated front panels. The pattern is typically Caucasian with stylized crab design, star pattern and flower and animal designs. Main border: flower and star design. Made in the 1920s.

SUMAKH (woven, not knotted)

Made in: the Caucasian district of Kuba in Azerbaijan and also near Derbent in the province of Daghestan.
Technique: herring-bone weave.
Warp: wool, in older carpets white, in newer ones brown.
Weft: dyed wool.
Pattern weave: fine quality wool.
Fringe: knotted and plaited fringe at either end.
Design: alternate large and small medallions and diamonds as well as small designs such as stars, "S", wine glass, hook and animals.
Colours: brown-red.
Sizes: mostly large sizes up to 10 ft. × 15 ft. approx. (300 × 450 cm.).
Azerbaijan usually produces a finer quality carpet than Daghestan.

Anatolian Karaman
4 ft. 7 in. × 8 ft. 11 in. approx.
(140 × 275 cm.).
Main design: lateral fields in different colours with all-over pattern of small rectilinear designs. Main border: stylized tree design at each end, zig-zag pattern and stylized flower design along the sides.

ANATOLIAN KELIM

Made in: Anatolia (Asia Minor).
Technique: Kelim weave with or without slits.
Warp: darkened or dyed wool.
Pattern weave: tightly spun wool.
Fringe: plaited or braided fringe at either end.
Design: as a rule in bands, different coloured fields, covered with small geometric motifs.
Colours: dark shades of dominating red, blue or yellow-white.
Sizes: small Kis-Kelim and up to 6 ft. 7 in. × 10 ft. approx. (200 × 300 cm.).
The largest sizes are generally woven in two parts that are then sewn together. The Kis-Kelims have very varied patterns, often with a niche design and other prayer rug patterns.

SEHNA-KELIM

Made in: the Persian city of Sehna (Sanandaj) and the neighbouring district.
Technique: Kelim weave with or without slits.
Warp: cotton.
Pattern weave: finely and tightly twisted wool.
Fringe: braided or ordinary fringe at either end.
Design: Herati design with or without medallion, also with niche design; this type is considered to be the foremost of all Kelims.
Colours: dominating dark colours in red, blue and yellow and with details in beige as a light element in the pattern.
Sizes: mostly about 3 ft. 9 in. × 5 ft. 7 in. approx. (110 × 170 cm.), but up to 4 ft. 6 in. × 8 ft. 4 in. approx. (135 × 250 cm.).

Sehna-Kelim   4 ft. 1 in. × 5 ft. 5 in. approx.
(124 × 165 cm.).
Main design: 3 stepped diamonds surrounded by stylized flower and leaf design. Main border: stylized flower design. Made in the 1930s.

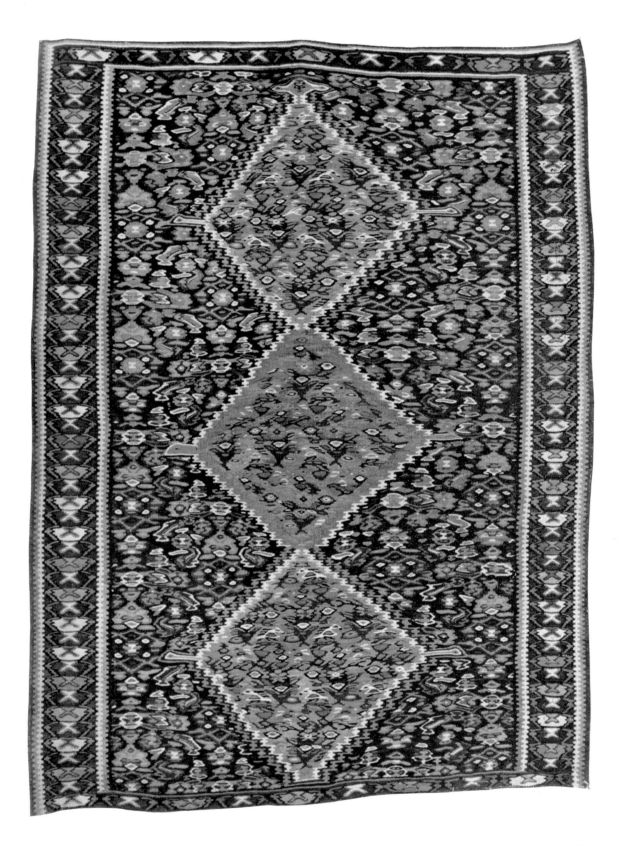

MERV-SUMAKH
AND MERV-PALLAS

Made in: the districts of Merv and Tekke in Turkestan.

Technique: Kelim weave or Sumakh technique.

Warp: wool or goats' hair.

Pattern weave: finely spun wool in Pallas, somewhat coarser and drier wool in Sumakh.

Fringe: plaited or braided fringe at either end.

Design: for Sumakh small diamond design in red and dark blue-green. For Pallas striped fields approximately 10-12 in. (25-30 cm.) wide in different colours; the field entirely monochrome or varied, so that part of the field has a geometrical pattern; also small geometrical diamonds or stepped design.

Colours: dark red, blue or green field.

Sizes: Sumakh up to 6 ft. 8 in. × 11 ft. 8 in. approx. (200 × 350 cm.); Pallas up to 5 ft. 11 in. × 11 ft. 8 in. approx. (180 × 350 cm.).

Merv-Sumakh 7 ft. × 11 ft. approx. (212 × 335 cm.).
Main design: all-over pattern of small diamonds.

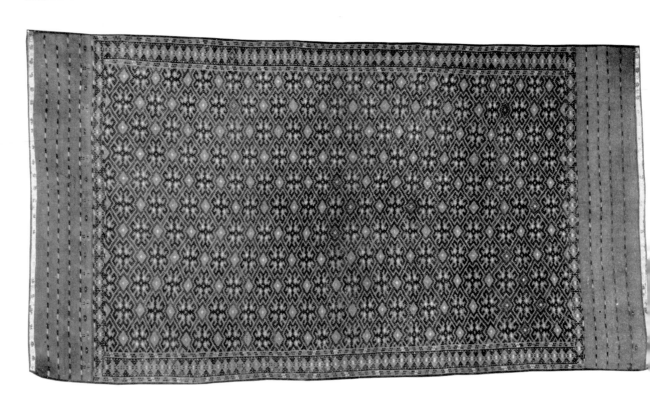

196

Merv–Pallas 4 ft. 5 in. × 7 ft. 11 in. approx. (135 × 245 cm.). Main design: cross and stepped pattern, completely rectilinear. Main border, zig-zag design. Made in the 1920s.

Kurdistan-Pallas

2 ft. 2 in. × 5 ft. 5 in. approx.
(70 × 165 cm.).

Main design: small diamond patterns in different colours placed in diagonal rows with small lateral "S" design. Main border: stylized arabesque and flower pattern. Made in the 1920s.

KURDISTAN-PALLAS

Made in: the district of Kurdistan in north-west Persia.

Technique: Kelim weave with or without slits.

Warp: wool or goats' hair or a mixture of both.

Pattern weave: tightly spun wool.

Fringe: plaited or braided fringe at either end.

Design: geometrical diamonds or lateral pattern with toothed octagons and zig-zag design. This type of Kelim is often woven in 2-3 strips that are then sewn together. Sometimes there are loose threads on the reverse side like those found with the Sumakh technique.

Colours: dark blue or red, but patterns with predominantly natural light colours are also found.

Sizes: up to 5 ft. 11 in. × 13 ft. 4 in. approx. (180 × 400 cm.).

Other Carpets

Buying a carpet
Looking after a carpet
Oriental terms

A large selection of carpets has already been described under each country but it has naturally not been possible to include all the existing types. Consequently, a brief account of the most important remaining carpets and their primary characteristics is given here.

Turkey

AK-HISSAR

Made in Anatolia, north-east of Izmir. Geometric patterns resembling Gendje.

BRUSA

South of Sea of Marmara. Silk rugs are very common, and prayer rugs.

DEMIRDJI

Near Ghiordes; Ghiordes and Kula patterns most common.

HOLBEIN

Made near Bergama. Older type, named after the painter Holbein.

KABA-KARAMAN

The town of Karaman in the district of Konya. Nomad production. Coarse knotting with Caucasian patterns. Karaman is also known for its production of Kelims.

KUMKAPU

Rare production of Armenian type. Extremely tightly knotted carpets, usually in silk.

PANDERMA

South of the Sea of Marmara. The Ghiordes pattern is most common with rough colours and harsh wool.

SIEBENBÜRGER

Probably Anatolian. Term for antique rugs found in this district. Patterns and qualities resemble those of the Bergama carpets.

SULTAN

Type resembling Yuruk (see page 66).

YASTIK

Made in many places in Turkey. The name simply refers to a small size, approx. 1 ft. 6 in. × 3 ft. (45 × 90 cm. approx.), or smaller.

Persia

ARDALAN

The Hamadan district. Recent type, flowing flower design.

ARMANIBAFF

Central area. The name means Armenian knotted. The types found on the market resemble both Luristan and Bahktiari. Mostly Ghiordes knot. Geometric patterns or Mir-Ibotha design, colours rather dark.

ASADABAD

Hamadan district. Mostly geometric patterns, such as diamond and rod medallions as well as stylized and leaf patterns. Ghiordes knot.

BIBIKABAD

Hamadan district. Rather thick and heavy quality with strongly contrasting colours and quite harsh wool. Patterns, stylized medallion and flower designs. Ghiordes knot.

BORCHALOU

Hamadan district. Flowing type of pattern with medallion and flower designs, mostly with a light beige ground. Ghiordes knot.

BURUJIRD

Central area. Patterns: the Mir-Ibotha pattern of the Seraband carpet and with Schekeri border, heavy type of wool. Ghiordes knot.

CHOREMABAD

Nomad type like Luristan, and from same area.

DERGEZIN

Hamadan district. The quality and type rather like Bibikabad except that the pattern is more naturalistic. Ghiordes knot.

ECKBATAN

Hamadan district. Thick and heavy. Pattern like Ardalan.

ELVEND

Hamadan district. Like Ardalan above, but somewhat heavier.

FERDOVS

Khurasan district. Patterns are mostly pointed medallions with a plain field, cochineal red colour.

GERUS

District of the same name. Type like Bijar, mostly all-over flower design arranged in rows.

GHARAGHAN

Kurdistan district. Heavy production, something between Bijar and Hamadan, mostly dark colours.

HUSEINABAD

Hamadan district. Thick and heavy type of quality. Patterns mostly geometrical. Medallion and flower designs. Ghiordes knot.

INJILAS

Hamadan district. Heavy type knotted with fine, lustrous wool and generally tighter than the other Hamadan qualities. Patterns: Mir-Ibotha, Herati designs. Ghiordes knot.

JORAGHAN

Hamadan district. Heavy type of wool. Patterns: stylized flower and bird design. Ghiordes knot. Not to be confused with Georavan in the Azerbaijan district.

JOZAN

Saruk district. Type like Saruk.

KARADAGH

District of the same name on the border with the Caucasus. Mostly gallery carpets with geometrical, stylized animal and flower designs.

KARAGHEUS

Hamadan district. Finer qualities, geometrical medallions and corners, reminiscent of the Feraghan carpets, and stylized flower design. The red colour often has a violet tint. Ghiordes knot.

KEMERE

Central area. Heavy type, geometrical medallions and stylized flower design. Ghiordes knot.

KHAMSEH

Hamadan district. Coarse Hamadan type. Patterns: rod medallion. Also the name for the nomad district north of Shiraz.

KOLTUK

Kurdistan district. Heavy type of wool. Herati-like pattern.

KOMAT

Iraq-Ajemi district. Medium thick quality. Stylized patterns. Rather dark colours. Ghiordes knot.

KOY

Azerbaijan district. The type resembles Tabriz but is more robustly made. Bird, tree and medallion designs.

LAVER-KERMAN

Also known as Raver-Kerman. Type like Kerman.

MASLAGHAN

Central. A rather special type of pattern with wedge-patterned medallions and corners clearly outlined against the ground. Ghiordes knot.

MESHKIN

Community near the Caucasian border, Azerbaijan district. Mostly gallery carpets, quite often in violet-red colours.

MEYGHAN

Central area. Massive and heavy quality somewhat reminiscent of Zendjan. Patterns: highly stylized flower and medallion patterns. Ghiordes knot.

MIANEH

South-east of Tabriz. Patterns: medallion and flower designs. Heavy wool, ribbed underside.

MIR

Central. These carpets are no longer made since the place was destroyed in an earthquake at the end of the 19th century. The type is now represented by the present Seraband but there is a very great difference in quality. The old Mir carpets still on the market are very expensive.

MORCHEKAR

North of Isfahan. Pattern resembling Joshagan.

MOSUL

Erroneous name for Hamadan carpet. The name comes from earlier exports via Mosul in Iraqi Kurdistan.

MUD

Khurasan district. Excellent quality. Usually Mir-Ibotha pattern but also medallion design.

MUSKABAD

Central. Mahal-like quality and mostly called this. Patterns, Herati, Guli Henna with or without medallion or corners. Sehna technique.

NAHAVAND

Near Malayer, and 75 miles (120 km.) east-south-east of Kermanshah. Typical Hamadan, with geometric design, usually all-over patterns. Ghiordes knot.

NIRIS

East of Shiraz. Type resembling Luristan. Naturalistic flower design, wool warp. A peculiarity is the ribbed underside.

POLONAISE CARPETS

Made in the 17th century in Isfahan and Kashan, later in Poland. Pattern type often with heraldic designs.

SAGHEH

Kurdistan district. Heavy type of wool but, even so, relatively densely knotted, geometrical patterns. Ghiordes knot.

SAHEND

Name for good quality new Tabriz carpets.

SARDERUD

Hamadan district. Relatively short pile, good wool. Patterns: stylized small designs with diamonds and medallions. Ghiordes knot.

SAVEH

West central area. Short pile, closely knotted, flower design and medallions. Often the patterns of the Maslaghan carpet. Ghiordes knot.

SERAPI

Heriz quality. Usually with cypress patterns.

SHAHSAVAN

Nomad tribe from south-east Persia, now living on the border between Kurdistan and Azerbaijan. Good carpets. The type resembles Hamadan.

SONGHUR

Kurdistan district. Heavy type reminiscent of Bijar with diamond and square patterns as well as stylized flower design. Ghiordes knot.

SOUTSCHBOLAG

Kurdistan district. Heavy type. Mostly crab and Mina-Khani design in original pattern.

TAFRESH

Central district, 50 miles (80 km.) west of Qum. Short pile. Flowing type of pattern with pointed medallions and very often bird design, mostly pastel shades. Both Ghiordes and Sehna knot.

TAIBAFF

Khurasan district. Excellent quality carpets.

TUISERKAN

Hamadan district. Relatively densely knotted, geometrical patterns. Ghiordes knot.

VERAMIN

South-east of Teheran. Qum-like quality. Mina-Khani patterns.

ZARAND

North-west of Kerman. The pattern either naturalistic flower designs or diamond-squared field over the whole field. Short pile. Ghiordes knot. Zarand is also the name of a town near Kerman.

ZIEGLER

The name of an English company that had large carpets made for export in Arak (Sultanabad). The typical Ziegler carpet has extremely few colours, mostly in pastel shades.

The Caucasus

CHICHI

Shirvan, Azerbaijan. Patterns and quality of pure Shirvan type, usually very small patterns.

DJABRAIL

Karabagh district. Usually large Mir-Ibotha patterns.

KABISTAN

Only a name in the trade for fine Shirvan carpets in the Kellei size. The name Kabistan probably comes from Kiaba-Shirvan = long-narrow Shirvan.

KAZAKJA

Small size of Kazak.

LESGHI

Daghestan district. Nomad quality. Patterns like others from Daghestan.

MUGHAN

Shirvan district. Usually a higher pile than in Shirvan carpets.

SCHUSCHA

Karabagh district. Like Karabagh but more loosely knotted.

TALISCH

Azerbaijan district. Mostly gallery size, geometrical patterns.

Turkestan

CHAUDOR

District in western Turkestan. The pattern is not the ordinary octagons but ovals in light and dark colours with small stylized flower and tree design. Flower tendrils round the ovals. Kabyrga border.

OGURDSCHALI

District in western Turkestan. Type like Chaudor but instead of ovals it has a pattern resembling the double eagle in the former Russian coat of arms and in contrasting colours. Kabyrga border.

There are many details that should be checked when buying a carpet. Some of them can be seen to at once, others must wait until the carpet has been taken home for a final look. Unfortunately, most buyers attach the greatest importance to exact colours and measurements. However, greater attention should be paid to quality, condition and pattern. A good carpet will in fact last a lifetime and should consequently be bought to be enjoyed as a work of art. Once again, let me repeat: rely only on reputable firms with long experience. You can then have confidence in your purchase. Buying at auctions and the like, with no chance of thoroughly checking the piece, can only be described as happy-go-lucky.

First check:

that the carpet lies flat on the floor; bulges or folds will lead to greater wear in those places and detract from the appearance of the carpet;

that the carpet is not too crooked; minor deviations should be accepted since this is a handicraft, particularly in the case of nomad carpets.

that the Kelim edges at the ends and the oversewing or braiding along the sides is not damaged, since these are intended to protect the knotted part of the carpet. Minor damage can easily be made good by a specialist without detracting from the carpet's value;

that the pattern is in harmony with the carpet's size in that there is no uncalled-for mutilation of the pattern at the border and that the patterns in the borders are so arranged at each corner that the harmony is maintained there as well.

After that, check the pile of the carpet. The surface should not be too uneven as a result of poor trimming or other factors.

Check the colours too. Make sure that the colours have not run into the light parts, that the surface of the pile has neither faded nor become excessively discoloured when compared with the colour inside. Nowadays there is not much risk of meeting aniline-dyed carpets, apart from some Turkish pieces and some older Indian carpets. Minor differences in colour between the surface and the foot of the pile may be tolerated.

By moistening the surface of the pile one can check a couple of points. If a lot of colour comes off when the surface is rubbed with a piece of

A genuine carpet is knotted.

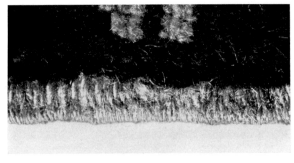

Uneven side edge (hand-sewn).

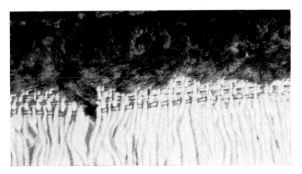

Machine-woven jute Wilton.

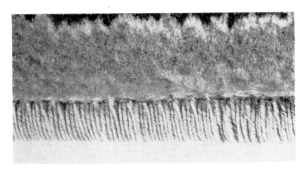

Even side edge, machine-sewn on a machine-woven carpet.

white linen, the colour is of inferior quality. Then one can smell the damp part of the carpet. A strong whiff of chlorine means that the carpet has been dry-cleaned and was probably rinsed badly after the treatment. This may mean a loss of durability. Excessively bleached carpets, so-called gold-Bokhara or gold-Afghan, may have a shorter lifetime after such treatment.

The next step is to inspect the underside of the carpet. First check the evenness of the knots, then whether the carpet has been repaired. This is easiest to see on the back. A minor repair properly done is no great disadvantage, but large repairs can affect the carpet's value.

Damage from moths on the underside will lay bare the warp in those places. As a result, the pile may work loose if the knot's anchorage has been eaten up by the moth.

The warp and the weft may be damaged as well but unfortunately this cannot always be seen.

Such damage may be due to one of two causes; either the yarn is too weak in relation to the carpet's weight or the carpet may have become damp and not been allowed to dry in a suitable manner.

To discover whether the weft is too weak or damaged, a rather extreme test can be made: fold back the carpet along a row of knots, then take hold of the folded carpet with both hands quite close to each other and pull both hands apart and downwards so as to bear on the weft threads. A cracking sound means that the wefts have broken, leaving a longitudinal split. Such a test must be made with the utmost care, preferably by a specialist.

Sometimes a carpet that is specially washed receives such hard treatment that certain colours, usually in plain fields, have to be touched up. This can be seen because the colour will not be evenly distributed over the pile and there will be a large difference in colour between the pile and the back of the carpet.

Knotted fringe on a genuine carpet.

Machine-woven carpet with fitted fringe.

How does one distinguish between genuine and imitation? Some of the most reliable indications are illustrated here.

A genuine carpet is knotted, the pile yarn is taken around one or more warp threads. This can be easily checked by folding the carpet vertically with the pile uppermost. The machine-woven jute Wilton is easily mistaken for a knotted carpet but no knots will be found at the bottom of the pile. The yarn runs loosely round the warp threads and can easily be pulled free.

The side edge of the genuine carpet is always somewhat uneven and wavy, with the yarn in several colours. The machine-woven carpet, on the other hand, has an even, straight side edge, which is attached after the carpet has been woven.

The fringe on a genuine carpet is always formed from the warp and may or may not be knotted. However, a machine-woven carpet can also have a fringe made from the warp, though generally the fringe has been finished. This gives the artificial appearance shown here.

Some carpets display belts of various widths in different shades, so-called "abrashes". There are several reasons for this. Several different batches of yarn may have been used, with some of them dyed a slightly different shade. Wool from different sheep may also take differently even though it is all dipped in the same dye bath. A large number of wide abrashes in one carpet is not particularly attractive but a few simply give the carpet a more lively appearance and consequently can be tolerated. However, these abrashes can hardly be controlled by the carpet-maker and will therefore be found even in the best qualities.

A carpet should be evaluated on the following grounds:

Density

The number of knots to the square inch or centimetre is highly relevant to a carpet's value, since the weavers are paid by the number of knots they tie. Wages are calculated to account for half a carpet's production costs.

Material

Naturally there is a difference in cost between good and inferior wool but the difference in price is relatively small in relation to the carpet's total cost.

Colours

There may be a great difference between the cost of synthetic dyes and the considerably more expensive vegetable dyes.

Labour

The details of the pattern can be executed skilfully or poorly. Sometimes the pattern is mutilated in order to keep the carpet within a certain size. This may affect both the field and the borders. What usually happens is that the border pattern does not fit at the ends and corners.

Pattern

A simple or mirror pattern costs less than, for instance, a figure pattern.

It should also be noted that high density knotting, good materials and vegetable dyes make the strongest carpets.

In the case of antique carpets, there is also age, history and condition to be considered.

THE CARPET AT HOME

When trying out a carpet at home, remember to turn it in different directions, since all carpets have one light and one dark aspect. When seen against the pile, the carpet appears darkest and the pattern stands out most clearly. Seen from the other direction, the carpet will appear much lighter.

There are places in the home for which a carpet should be chosen primarily from the point of view of durability and the practical necessity of having a carpet of which one does not grow tired and that is easy to look after.

A carpet for the hall should preferably be heavy and robust, i.e., durable, while one for a dining-room should have a dense, short pile since this is more practical and easy to look after.

Carpets with light colours are generally more practical than dark ones and an over-all pattern is more practical than a large, plain field.

As a general rule, carpets with a cotton warp lie better than those with a warp of wool or goats' hair. This disadvantage, however, can be eliminated by using a suitable undercarpet. A carpet with a cotton warp will not wear so well.

When faced with a choice between an older carpet and a newer one, choose the former, because in most cases there will probably be greater value in a product on which more time has been spent. Moreover, age will have given the carpet a certain prestige.

Experience has shown that many carpets become worn out or damaged too early owing to bad handling. Here, then, is some simple advice about caring for your carpets.

During the first months a new carpet should definitely not be beaten and preferably not vacuum cleaned, at any rate not too often. This is because the pile should first be trod well in, since this makes the surface less liable to wear.

A new carpet will moult a certain amount, depending on the length of its pile but this does not affect the quality or lifetime and will gradually cease. In wool piles, it is the short fibres that moult, leaving mostly the shiny top hair, so that a carpet develops its proper sheen only after a certain amount of wear. Never try to pull out knots or thick threads; let an expert cut or fasten them.

If it becomes essential to beat a carpet, this should be done with a broad-bladed beating stick, not with an ordinary rattan or wooden stick. Otherwise, the fine warp or weft threads are easily broken, leaving a hole. Always beat the carpet from behind. The dust will then work out on to the top of the pile, from where it is easily removed with a dry brush used "with the pile".

When vacuum cleaning, make sure that the mouthpiece is smooth; always work in the direction of the pile, so that the dust is not pressed back into the carpet. It is wrong to continue vacuum cleaning for as long as fluff keeps on coming into the cleaner, since in this way it is possible to destroy the carpet's pile entirely.

Spots of dirt and fat should be removed with volatile cleaning agents: petrol or carbon tetrachloride. Always use a clean rag, and make sure that it is done in a well-ventilated room or out of doors to avoid the fumes from these liquids. Spots that are difficult to remove or a thoroughly dirty carpet should be washed by a specialist. Do not try to clean the carpet with, for instance, damp tea leaves, a wet rag or the like. The dust will only become moist and fasten more firmly in the carpet, the colours will loose their freshness and the carpet will look shabby.

If moths are suspected, use suitable insecticide, carefully inspect the entire carpet, use the beater

A genuine carpet should be washed at a recognized establishment which has experience of this work and special apparatus for the purpose.

and vacuum cleaner and leave it to lie for hours in the sun and fresh air. Extensive moth damage may make it necessary to have the carpet washed, disinfected and moth-proofed at the same time. This is not particularly expensive but is extremely effective.

A ragged fringe or side is not only unsightly but also easily leads to the edge being torn. It is therefore best to have any damage mended as soon as possible. A good way of prolonging the lifetime of a carpet is to use a foundation of sponge rubber or moth-proofed, honeycomb felt with a rubber base. This also prevents the carpet from sliding about, which is not only annoying but can be dangerous. The foundation should of course be slightly smaller than the carpet to avoid the foundation from being seen outside the edges.

When scrubbing or washing the floor, do not fold the carpet but roll it up. Moreover, make sure that the floor is quite dry before putting back the carpet as otherwise it will absorb the moisture and easily become mouldy and brittle. Do not polish the floor underneath the carpet as the polish may give rise to spots that are impossible to remove.

Remember that the lifetime of a carpet is very largely dependent upon the treatment it receives. Treated properly and carefully, it will last longer. Investing capital in a fine, hand-woven carpet is investing in a work of art.

In the carpet trade one can both read and hear completely misleading terms of various kinds used by ignorant salesmen to impress customers. One example is when a carpet is called a Zar(o)nim. This is not the name for a carpet but simply the oriental term for the size approximately 3 ft. 4 in. × 5 ft. (100 × 150 cm.). The term can be used regardless of the district from which the carpet comes, and of course a carpet should also be given the name of the district where it is made. Moreover, there are a number of double names; some are justified, e.g., Pendic-Bokhara or Hatchlou-Afghan, but terms such as Princess-Bokhara or Royal-Kashan are far too specific to be relied on, since they may well be mis-applied by salesmen with insufficient knowledge. The additional terms are, of course, meant to emphasise the extra high quality of the carpet.

Another misleading term is Mecca-Shiraz. In fact, no Shiraz carpets are made in Mecca and this is simply a means of indicating a high quality and thereby justifying a higher price.

Laver-Kerman is often heard in the trade as a name for an older, thinner type of Kerman.

Laver is not a place but simply indicates a better quality than the ordinary Kerman. This may be a case of confusion with Ravar, north of Kerman, where very fine qualities used to be made.

Here, finally, are some terms with their explanations as well as some terms for sizes and patterns. Note that in the West, the term "rug" is used to denote pieces up to 8 ft. × 4 ft. approx. (244 × 122 cm.); anything larger is called a "carpet".

Approximate sizes:

YASTIK	1 ft. 5 in. × 2 ft. 9 in. approx. (45 × 90 cm.).
PUSHTI	.. 2 ft. × 2 ft. 9 in. approx. (60 × 90 cm.).
ZARQUART	2 ft. × 4 ft. 1 in. approx. (60 × 125 cm.).
ZAR(O)NIM	3 ft. 4 in. × 5 ft. approx. (100 × 150 cm.).
SEDJADEH	4 ft. 3 in. × 5 ft. 10 in. approx. (130 × 180 cm.).
DOZAR	4 ft. 7 in. × 6 ft. 7 in. approx. (140 × 200 cm.).
PERDE	5 ft. × 7 ft. 2 in. approx. (150 × 220 cm.).
KIABA	5 ft. 7 in. × 8 ft. 10 in. approx. (170 × 270 cm.), or longer.
KELLEI	5 ft. 7 in. × 8 ft. 10 in. approx. (170 × 270 cm.), or longer.
KENAREH	Gallery shape. Runners of about 10 or 11 ft. (304 or 335 cm.).
MAKATLYK	Gallery shape. Runners of about 10 or 11 ft. (304 or 335 cm.).

Names of patterns:

GULI or GUL	Flower.
HATCH	Cross.
MAH	Moon.
MAHI	Fish.
MIHRAB	Niche.

Names indicative of the carpet's use:

BERDELYK	Wall carpet (decoration).
CHURDJIN	Small saddle bag.
ENESSI	Door (tent) drapery.
HAMAMLYK	Bathmat.
HEHBELYK	Saddle cover.
MAFRASH	Large saddle bag.
NAMASLYK	Prayer rug.
NAMAZI	Prayer rug.
SAFF	Family prayer rug.
TORBA	Storage bag.
TSCHOVAL	Large storage bag.
TURBEHLYK	Grave rug.

Miscellaneous:

ABRASH	Multi-coloured field.
AGRAB	Scorpion.
BAFF	Knot.
BAREH	Lamb.
BOZGALEH	Goat.
BOZORG	Large.
DJUFT	Pair.
DO-RUJA	Double-sided.
ESKI	Ancient.
FARSIBAFF	Persian knot.
GHALI	Carpet.
GUSSFAND	Sheep.
KARAGHEUS	Black eye (carpet name, Persia).
KAR-HENE	Mat factory.
KIS	Small, also girl (Turkey).
KUCHEK	Small (Persia).
KUH	Mountain.
KUMKAPU	Sandstreet (name of carpet, Turkey).
RUD	River.
SHIRAZI	Edge inspection.
SHOTOR	Camel.
TALIM	Cartoon or pattern plan.
TURKBAFF	Turkish knot.

COLOUR PHOTOGRAPHS

MAPS

PHOTOGRAPHERS

Colour photographs: Pan Studio
Black and white photographs of rugs: Allfoto, Esselte Foto
and Pan Studio
Separate black and white photographs:
Antikvarisk Topografiska Arkivet (p. 10)
Ben Eriksson, IMS (p. 208, 209)
Dagens Bild (p. 212)
Lennart Olson, TIO (p. 22, 28)
Victoria & Albert Museum, Crown Copyright (p. 11, 178)